Perfect Written English

Chris West has been a professional writer for many years. He has written fiction, including *Death of a Blue Lantern*, travel (*Journey to the Middle Kingdom*) and non-fiction, where he is best known as co-author of the bestselling *The Beermat Entrepreneur*. He has written for the business press, authoring a column in *Director* magazine for five years, and reviewed travel books for the *Independent on Sunday*. Chris has also worked in marketing and PR, writing copy, press releases and ghosted press pieces, and as a writing and communications trainer. Married, with one daughter, he lives near Cambridge.

More details on www.chriswest.info

Other titles in the *Perfect* series

Perfect
Written English

Chris West

BOOKS

Published by Random House Books 2008

2 4 6 8 10 9 7 5 3 1

First published in Great Britain in 2008 by
Random House Books

Random House Books
Random House, 20 Vauxhall Bridge Road,
London SW1V 2SA

www.rbooks.co.uk

Addresses for companies within The Random House Group Limited
can be found at: www.randomhouse.co.uk/offices.htm

The Random House Group Limited Reg. No. 954009

A CIP catalogue record for this book
is available from the British Library

ISBN 9781847945037

The Random House Group Limited makes every effort to ensure that the
papers used in its books are made from trees that have been legally sourced
from well-managed and credibly certified forests. Our paper procurement
policy can be found at: www.rbooks.co.uk/environment

Mixed Sources
Product group from well-managed
forests and other controlled sources
www.fsc.org Cert no. TT-COC-2139
© 1996 Forest Stewardship Council

FSC

Typeset in Minion by Palimpsest Book Production Limited,
Grangemouth, Stirlingshire
Printed and bound in the UK by CPI Bookmarque, Croydon CR0 4TD

Contents

'Everything that can be said, can be said clearly'

Ludwig Wittgenstein

Introduction

I love that quote from Wittgenstein. When I'm ploughing through some ghastly corporate report, impenetrable piece of academic postmodern-speak or someone's unpunctuated, mis-spelt email, I look up and imagine the great philosopher's words shining out like a beacon of hope. We are not fated to drown in a sea of illiteracy. Good writing matters, and always will matter.

But the tide of poor writing does seem to be rising. My personal bugbear is 'managementese':

> *In this document a number of initiatives are subjected to an examination process with respect both to viability and ongoing strategic relevance . . .*

This empty, heartless gobbledegook is now written – and even spoken – in big business, in government and (of all places!) in education.

Of course there are other sorts of bad writing, too. Dull writing, ambiguous writing, downright incomprehensible writing, writing that shows a failure to master the basics of grammar and punctuation, writing so full of padding you want to pop it with a pin, writing that wanders aimlessly, writing that deliberately obfuscates in order to deceive. All such writing is at best impolite and at worst dangerous. Dangerous? On a simple level, it's dangerous because it is unclear, and can thus misinform or misdirect. At a deeper level, it's dangerous because it encourages dim-witted conformity. Clear thinking and the ability to communicate those thoughts effectively are powerful weapons in the hands of those who want to question and change things, or of those who wish to question misguided change. A society where stupidity is patronised and intelligence becomes equated with the ability to spew out jargon – well, George Orwell got there well over half a century before I did: such a society is the hellish world of *1984* and *Animal Farm*.

Never mind. This book isn't a rant, but a handbook for change. We can all do something about this. You've started, by picking up this book. I hope you'll enjoy working through it, and that you'll keep on referring to it as you develop your skills in our beautiful, subtle, expressive and infinitely valuable language. As you do so, take pride in standing up for what is good, strong and lasting against what is meretricious, enfeebling and cheap. The revolution starts here!

1 Parts of speech, groups of words, parsing

Like all revolutionaries, we need to get some basic training in first. So off to boot camp!

You're allowed to groan at this point. My students normally do. 'We did all this stuff at school!' That's just what I thought when I decided to teach writing and sat down to create a course in what I thought I already knew – and found that there was a huge amount that I only half understood. Those basic lessons have helped me a great deal in all my writing ever since.

Individual words (also called 'parts of speech')

Let's begin by classifying words. First, the four easiest ones:

Nouns are things, places or concepts. *Cat, London, patience.* Most nouns can be singular (*a cat*) or plural (*two or more cats*).

Verbs are actions or descriptions of states. *Go, remember, have.* Verbs are grammatically the most complex words; they come in all sorts of forms: tenses, 'voices', 'moods' . . . A book like this can only scrape the surface of this complexity. Verbs lie at the heart of lively writing, and have taken a particularly terrible battering from managementese. (More on this later.)

Adjectives tell us something about (or 'qualify', in the jargon) nouns (**blue** *sky*, **happy** *face*).

Adverbs tell us something about verbs (*ran* **quickly**, *coming* **soon**) or adjectives (*he was* **grossly** *fat*).

Being pernickety, what we're really talking about is word *roles*. A simple word like *round* can play the role of a noun, verb, adjective, adverb or, jumping ahead, a preposition.

> *You bought the drinks last time; now it's my round.* (noun)
>
> *The tiger suddenly rounded on its trainer.* (verb)
>
> *The world is round.* (adjective)
>
> *He looked round, but still couldn't see if he was being followed.* (adverb)
>
> *The Countess showed me round the house herself.* (preposition)

Standard practice is to refer to words as 'parts of speech' rather than as playing roles – in other words we say, 'In example one, *round* is a noun,' rather than, 'In example one, *round* is playing a noun role,' which would be more accurate. To keep things simple and clear, I'm going to stick to standard practice.

After the 'big four', it gets a bit more complex.

Pronouns 'stand in' for nouns in various ways. Don't worry too much about the names, but just note the variety of pronouns.

- Personal pronouns: *I, you, he, she* etc., but also *me* and *mine*.

- Demonstrative pronouns, so called because they are often used when showing something, as in **This** *is my book*.

- Interrogative pronouns, which ask questions: *Where am I?*

- Relative pronouns, which relate groups of words to nouns, as in *The person **who** did that.*

- There are also 'indefinite' pronouns – words like *nobody, either.*

Note, again, that a word can 'be' more than one kind of pronoun. *That* is a demonstrative pronoun in ***That's** mine!* and a relative pronoun in *The idea **that** I had yesterday.*

Two useful pieces of terminology:

- The noun for which a pronoun is standing in is called its 'antecedent'.

- The standing-in process is called 'referring to'. In *Here's Anna. She is my cousin*, the pronoun *she* is said to 'refer to' Anna.

Conjunctions link words, usually of similar types, for example two nouns *(bread **and** jam)* or two adjectives *(she was pretty **but** shallow).* Conjunctions can also link groups of words: *Since you were going to London, **and** I had to leave for Bristol at the same time, we shared a taxi.*

Please ignore the hoary old maxim that you cannot begin a sentence with a conjunction. Rubbish! The conjunction at the start of *And finally, I'd like to thank Mrs Jones . . .* is simply linking the new sentence to something that has gone before.

Prepositions link words, as conjunctions do, but in a more purposeful way. They often say something about how, why, when or where something happened. For example:

*The car was removed **by** the police.* (how)

*The car was removed **by** mistake.* (why)

*I want that car removed **by** four o'clock . . .* (when)

*. . . and left **by** the garage, where it belongs.* (where)

Prepositions often link nouns to other parts of the sentence (***by** the police, **by** the garage* etc.). In this case the technical term is that the noun (*the police, the garage*) is 'governed' by the preposition.

Determiners come in front of nouns. This is a new category since I learned grammar at school, which shows that the subject is not static. Rather than go into elaborate detail, I'll just say that there are various types of determiner. Examples of determiners are what used to be called 'quantifiers' – ***some** eggs,* **no** *problem,* ***every** time,* ***all** people that on earth do dwell* – and the definite and indefinite articles, *the* and *a*.

The two articles, *the* and *a*, may seem mundane, but they have a quiet power. *A car* means one of all the cars out there; which one is not specified (hence the name *indefinite* article). *The car* implies we are talking about a specific, *definite* vehicle. This focuses our attention more – we're talking about a particular one.

> ***A** car went past the window.* We haven't heard of this car before. We don't know anything else about it, and may not hear of it again.

> ***The** car went past the window.* What car? We've obviously heard of it before, and probably should know something about it. We'll probably hear more about it, too.

It's a trick that crime writers use, to put in among a whole lot of defined things something apparently undefined like *a car went past the window.* Readers are naturally concentrating on the defined objects, and forget the car – which later turns out to be a key clue. But this is, of course, a deliberate game. If you want to be clear, and this book is all about clarity, use the correct article to send the correct signal to the reader.

I could go into the topic of parts of speech in endless depth, but there's no point here – if you're interested, there are plenty of good books on the subject. The most important things are:

- Understand the basics outlined above
- Don't worry too much about the technicalities.

Groups of words

If the word is the basic unit of sense in a piece of writing, the unit at the next level up is the sentence. We all know what a sentence is, don't we?

No. Double-checking when writing this book, I looked in various sources and found totally different definitions. One said 'anything beginning with a capital letter and ending in a proper mark (usually a full stop, but sometimes an exclamation or question mark)'. Another defined a sentence as a group of words 'complete in itself'. A third said it was 'a group of words containing a verb'.

There's sense in all of these, actually. Combining them, I say that a sentence is something that:

- begins with a capital letter
- ends with a proper mark
- contains a verb.

By implication, such a group of words would be 'complete in itself'.

Technically, a sentence has to include a *finite* verb. A finite verb is a verb that has a subject (this is discussed in more depth in the next section). But don't lose too much sleep over this. I never have.

There are other useful terms for other groups of words.

A group of words without a finite verb is a **phrase**. *The purple lorry came slowly down the hill* is a sentence. In that sentence, *the purple lorry* is a phrase, as is *slowly down the hill*.

Phrases can do the jobs of nouns (***loving you*** *is easy*), of adverbs (*the meals arrived* ***right on time***), or of adjectives (***delirious with joy***, *he leapt into the Thames*).

A **fragment** is a phrase dressed up as a sentence – in other words beginning with a capital and ending with a full stop, but lacking a finite verb. Tony Blair's speeches, especially at the start of his time as PM, were full of these. 'New Labour. *(Pause)* New Britain. *(Pause)* New future.' (And so on.) So are certain types of advert. 'You need your mail delivered. Promptly. Politely.' (A sentence plus two fragments.) Fragments are useful for emphasising points, but become very irritating when overused.

A **clause** is a group of words that contains a finite verb but is not a fully fledged sentence (it has no capital at the start or no full stop at the end). There are two types of clause – main and subordinate. Main clauses make sense on their own; subordinates don't. In the sentence *The cat sat on the mat which I cleaned yesterday*, the words *the cat sat on the mat* are the main clause, while *which I cleaned yesterday* is a subordinate clause.

In this example, *sat*, the verb in the main clause, is called the 'main verb', while *cleaned* is called a 'dependent verb'. If a sentence is formed by joining two main clauses (*the cat sat on the mat and left a load of fleas*), there are two main verbs.

Subordinate clauses, like phrases, can do the work of parts of speech. They can act as nouns (***What I like about you*** *is your* *sense of humour*), as adverbs (*He opened the letter **when I told him to***) or as adjectives (*He finally met Sally, **who had become his sister's best friend at uni***). This last type of subordinate clause, telling us something more about a noun, is also called a 'relative clause'.

All these – phrases, fragments, clauses – are smaller than (or sometimes equal to) sentences. There are, of course, groups of words bigger than a sentence. The next unit up is the paragraph. But let's leave such things for the moment and take a closer look at how sentences work.

Taking sentences to bits . . .

. . . is called **parsing**. The classic formula I learned was 'subject, verb, object, everything else'. In the sentence *The cat ate the mouse, The cat* is the subject, *ate* is the verb and the unfortunate *mouse* is the object. If we expand our sentence to *The cat ate the mouse, licking its lips in between bites in a rather unpleasant manner*, then *licking its lips in between bites in a rather unpleasant manner* is just 'everything else'. Grammarians will no doubt throw their hands up in horror at this, but it's always worked for me.

It is useful to understand the difference between two types of **object** – direct and indirect. In the sentence *She gave the book to Uncle Fred*, the book is the direct object (the thing that she gave) and Uncle Fred is the indirect object (the person to whom the book was given).

Another key term in parsing is the **complement**. This is what follows verbs that are about 'states' rather than actions. *To be* is the obvious 'state' verb. If you say *I am a writer*, *I* is clearly the subject and *am* is clearly the verb, but it feels a little odd to call *a writer* the object. 'Object' implies being on the receiving end of something, rather than just being a state. So we call *a writer* in this sentence the complement. Note that complements can also be adjectives. *I am* **hungry** – subject, verb, complement. Other examples of 'state' verbs followed by complements might be *I feel* **unwell**; *the weather remains* **glorious**; *Gemma looked* **radiant** *in her new outfit*; *he will become* **an inspector** *next week*.

Finally, note the distinction between **simple and complex sentences**. Simple sentences are basically just main clauses. *I went out for half an hour.* Complex sentences are a main clause plus one or more subordinate clauses and/or one or more main clauses joined to it. Examples:

> Two main clauses. *He slammed the door and went out into the rain.*
>
> Main plus subordinate. *He slammed the door, which made the jug fall off the shelf.*
>
> Two mains plus subordinate. *He slammed the door, which made the jug fall off the shelf, and went out into the rain.*

Good writers are masters of complex sentences, though over the years sentences have tended to become simpler, even in literary writing, no doubt due to the increased pace we expect in everything nowadays. I'll return to this notion when I talk about style (see Chapter 7).

This chapter has been brief, but has, I hope, introduced or clarified a number of concepts essential to writing good English. To conclude it, please run through this list and make sure you understand the definitions of:

- nouns

- verbs

- adjectives
- adverbs
- pronouns, antecedents, pronouns 'referring to' nouns
- conjunctions
- prepositions
- determiners and articles (definite and indefinite)
- sentences (simple and complex)
- phrases
- fragments
- clauses (main, subordinate and relative)
- subject
- object (direct and indirect)
- complement.

Got them? Good. Time to move on.

2 Punctuation

Previously regarded as strictly for professional writers or pedants, this topic suddenly became sexy thanks to Lynne Truss's *Eats, Shoots and Leaves*. People who had long repressed the desire to rush out and correct signs saying 'Potatoe's 50p' could now come out of the closet and admit their compulsion with pride.

My own approach is a little less rigid than Lynne Truss's (her book bears the strapline 'The Zero Tolerance Approach to Punctuation'). But only a little. There are rules, and they need to be adhered to.

The most important thing to understand about punctuation is that it's not some kind of test, but a tool to make your writing clearer. If you could write crystal-clear prose that used no punctuation at all, that would be fine. Sadly, however, you can't.

Another 'big four'

There are four main punctuation marks, and they exist in an order of magnitude. From lowest to highest they are:

- comma

- semicolon

- colon

- full stop.

Think of them as 'units of pause'. A comma is one unit, a semicolon two units, a colon three units, and a full stop is four. Or, more subtly, a semicolon is two units and a colon two-and-a-half, jumping to four for the full stop.

Not everybody agrees with this. The 'units of pause' idea is regarded as too simple, particularly failing to capture the subtle differences between the semicolon and the colon. Of course, the purists are right: things are more complex than the 'units' model – but the model is easy to use and captures a large slice of the truth about these marks, so I like it. Like many simple rules, you can jettison it once you've mastered it. I must admit I still find it helpful.

Let's look at the big four marks in increasing order:

The **comma** is the basic unit of pause. Its main use is to divide a complex sentence into its basic parts.

> *I will arrive tomorrow, if that is convenient for you.*
>
> *By capitalising expenses such as research or certain types of training, one can make the balance sheet of a company look much healthier than it actually is.*

In the first example, the comma is grammatically necessary, as it separates two clauses, one main and one subordinate. In the second it is a politeness to the reader, indicating the correct point to pause in a long, and rather weighty, sentence.

Commas are also used for bracketing off non-essential parts of a sentence, bits that add titbits of extra information rather than provide the main message:

Mr Jones, who seemed to be in a great hurry, ran past without saying hello.

The computers, initially installed three weeks late, were already beginning to malfunction.

The treasure, however, was never found.

In all the above examples, try taking the bracketed words out – the sentence still makes its point.

Remember that if you bracket with commas, you must close the brackets:

Wrong: *The car, sorry to say was in a mess when it was brought back.*

Right: *The car, sorry to say, was in a mess when it was brought back.*

A comma is needed when a sentence is turned round so that a subordinate clause is put before a main clause:

Before turning on the zoomatron, please read the instructions.

But:

Please read the instructions before turning on the zoomatron.

The comma can be used for emphasis:

Emma came into the room, slowly.

Take the comma away, and what matters is that Emma came in, not how she did it, which is a kind of afterthought. For a more melodramatic effect, use a dash – but remember that melodrama is a hair's breadth away from self-parody.

Commas can protect a sentence from ambiguity (and from looking downright silly):

> *Lord Snodsbury said he had shot himself as a young*
> *man.*

So he was a zombie? Much more likely, His Lordship mentioned that he'd blasted off at a few pheasants when he was a lad. In other words:

> *Lord Snodsbury said he had shot, himself, as a young*
> *man.*

Watch out for lone commas. They sometimes rove around bad writing and just settle down wherever they feel like it. Commas shouldn't separate subjects and verbs:

> *Emma, came into the room slowly.*

If the writer of the above put the comma in thinking he was emphasising Emma, he was wrong. To emphasise it, try:

> *It was Emma who came into the room slowly.*

Or:

> *Everybody else raced into the room. Emma came in*
> *slowly.*

Lone, lost commas are usually there because the writer got a fit of jitters that the sentence was 'too long' not to have one. There's a myth that every sentence should have one comma. That's absurd. However, it is true that most long sentences improve with a comma in the right place. The comma shows where the *pivot* of the sentence is. Maybe a helpful rule is that every sentence over 20 words long ought to have a comma.

The pivot of a sentence

This is a useful notion, but one that's hard to pin down. It's the point at which a sentence turns.

The cat sat on the mat has no pivot.

The cat sat on the mat and fell asleep has the pivot at *and*, which is joining two main clauses. (Pivots often come at conjunctions, as anyone who's been told *I love you, but . . .* will know.)

Sentences describing things unfolding over time pivot at the time change. *Emma came into the room, quickly for once, and gave a gasp* pivots at *and*.

Long sentences usually have a pivot in them somewhere – if they don't, they are almost guaranteed to be unbearably dull.

One way to find the pivot is to read the sentence out loud, and notice where you naturally pause.

On the subject of myths, here's another one. 'You never put a comma before *and*.' Rubbish! If you think it would help the reader to get the gist of the sentence quickly and easily, then put a comma before *and* and do so with pride. Consider the sentence:

*We left early, took the train, and were in London by
10.30.*

I like the comma before the *and*, because the real pivot of the
sentence is between *We left early and took the train* and *We were in
London* a while later.

However, it is standard practice to leave the comma out before
and:

We set out knives, forks and spoons

is correct, not *knives, forks, and spoons*. But use common sense.
If the list is of complex things, a comma before the *and* can
help:

*We set out golden knives with the family crest on, some
special forks with eight prongs, and an array of
glistening silver spoons*

is much clearer than the comma-less *and*. Without the comma
the reader might think that what was coming after the *and* was
something else you were going to say about the forks, rather than
introducing the next class of utensil. This extra comma before the
and is known as the serial, or 'Oxford', comma. I don't know why.

Remember, punctuation is not a test, but a guide for the reader,
and a guiding principle in the debate about commas in lists of
adjectives is feel. Standard practice is to have them, so:

The castle was a shabby, overgrown ruin.

This usage highlights the adjectives, and tells the reader that each
adjective matters. But if the adjectives are less important and really

only there for form's sake, then commas look odd. You don't sing 'The grand, old Duke of York'.

One rule that really is unbreakable is the one that says you shouldn't use commas to join main clauses with different subjects. It's fine to write:

> *I went to town, bought a suit and came home*

but not:

> *I went to town, you were on the same train too.*

The comma is too weak a pause for this: readers need to know there's a serious shift in sense coming up, to say to themselves, 'There's one unit of information, and now here's a different unit of information.' The job for this sort of break goes to the semicolon.

The **semicolon** is the most underused punctuation mark around. Many business reports and even some business books have none at all. This sets alarm bells ringing with me – if the writer can't use one of the basic tools of the trade, are they going to be able to use any of the others? (But apparently Orwell hated semicolons, and he is one of the great prose writers of the last century.)

Look at older writing, and it will often be littered with semicolons where we would now use commas. Here's Gerald Winstanley, writing at the time of the Civil War:

> *In the beginning of Time Man had Domination given to him over the Beasts; but not one word was spoken that one branch of mankind should rule over another.*

Now we'd probably just have a comma before *but*. I don't think this means the semicolon needs to be added to the list of endangered species, along with the white rhinoceros and the Bengal tiger. It does mean the mark has found a narrower set of uses, all of which will continue to be valuable.

One of these, as we've seen above, is for joining two main clauses with different subjects:

> *I went to town; you were on the same train too.*

This is best done where the two clauses 'deserve' to be linked – in other words, when there's something to be gained from linking them. If the sentences are unconnected, then the semicolon link is wrong; just keep them as separate sentences:

> *I went to Totnes. England lost three wickets before
> lunch.*

In a long sentence full of subordinate clauses and phrases, and thus commas, the semicolon tells the reader where the pivot is.

> *He got out of the car, which he had parked untypically
> badly, and noticed Jane, the very person he needed to
> talk to, walking along the pavement with her usual
> slow, pensive gait; but instead of calling out to her, he
> looked the other way, muttered something into his
> beard and blushed.*

The semicolon is also needed in lists, where descriptive phrases requiring commas get muddled up with each other:

The luggage included a trunk, all covered in stickers;
two packages, one brown and one green; red, white and
blue flags; a flight case once used by Emerson, Lake
and Palmer; a plastic bag.

Without semicolons, this is hell:

The luggage included a trunk, all covered in stickers,
two packages, one brown and one green, red, white and
blue flags, a flight case once used by Emerson, Lake
and Palmer, a plastic bag.

Stylists say that the semicolon 'promises more' – when you see one in the middle of a sentence, you know there's more substantial information coming your way before the sentence ends.

The **colon** is a slightly bigger divider than the semi. It's used:

*   To introduce lists:

    These are the traits we value: ambition, intelligence and
    sociability.

*   To express contrast, especially in snappy expressions where the two halves of the contrast balance perfectly:

    United we stand: divided we fall.

(Note that the semicolon can also be used for contrast. For sentences where the contrast is less succinct, a semicolon is often better. But there's no clear rule here: develop your own style.)

- When the second half of a sentence clarifies the first half rather than tells us something radically new:

  The comma is too weak a pause for this: the reader needs to know there's a serious shift in sense coming up.

(As with the contrast above, a semicolon would not be wrong in this example – I just prefer the colon here.)

- When a sentence builds up to a piece of information:

  There's only one way Emma ever entered rooms: slowly.

  There's one problem with getting Helen and Anna to work together on this project: they can't stand one another.

This kind of use is 'rhetorical' – to get a laugh or achieve a rhetorical effect – and is often found in speeches or pamphlets.

- The colon is also used to introduce a formal quote.

  As Shakespeare said: 'All the world's a stage'.

(Note that you sometimes see a 'colon and dash' mark :– This makes a cute nose and eyes for text messaging, but has no role these days as a piece of punctuation.)

The **full stop** is less complex than the above marks. End of the sentence. Period. (That's what the Americans call it, a 'period'.)

The full stop also has some odd uses: in abbreviations like etc. (= *et cetera*) and i.e. (as in *Recent staff, i.e. those who joined since 2002, are invited to meet the chairman*). It used to be used a lot more, in abbreviations like Mr, Dr, Rev, Jan, Feb, Mar, Mon, Tues,

Wed (etc.) and in acronyms like NATO, BBC, USA; but in all these cases its use has faded.

And the rest . . .

Other punctuation marks are a lot less important. Rather than go into them in enormous detail, I shall just make a few comments.

Apostrophes look amateurish if you get them wrong. Their correct use is for possessives (*Joanna's desk*) and where words have been contracted (*don't*). The classic misuse is in plurals – the famous 'greengrocers' apostrophe':

> *Potatoe's 30p*
>
> *Carrot's 60p*

Please avoid, especially if you are a greengrocer. You don't want to be stereotyped, do you?

Just to remind any readers unsure of the rule: *No* plural takes the –*'s* form. *Ever*. The plural of *cat* is *cats*. If you see *cat's*, it has one of two meanings:

> *The cat's tail was waving.* (possessive – the tail *of the cat*)
>
> *The cat's gone out.* (contraction, standing for *the cat has gone out*)

Other apostrophe problems occur with:

- It's and its.

The lion ate its dinner. (possessive)

It's raining! (contraction of *it is*)

This isn't logical. In the cat example above, *cat's* is both possessive and a contraction, so why isn't *it's* used in both cases? Answer: nobody knows. But that's how it is. *It's* is the contraction; *its* is the possessive. (Moral: while the rules of language are largely logical, the logic is frayed at the edges. Language is perpetually evolving, and ease of use and euphony are bigger drivers of change than logic.)

- Who's and whose. **Whose** *coat is this?* (possessive) but **Who's** *left a coat behind?* (contraction of 'who has'). Or *The man* **whose** *coat I took by mistake* (relative pronoun) and *The man* **who's** *coming to collect it tomorrow* (contraction of 'who is').

- Possessives of singular nouns ending in s. *Keats's poems* or *Keats' poems*? I prefer the latter, which follows the rule for the possessives of plurals, most of which end in –s and which do not take a second 's' – *The three cats' greatest enemy was the dog three houses down*, not *The three cats's . . .*

- The possessives of phrases, which people get very tied up with – for example how do you write 'the house of Nick and Annie'? *Nick and Annie's house* or *Nick's and Annie's house*? The latter feels more democratic, but actually the former is correct, unless Nick and Annie each own separate items, rather than share ownership of one item, in which case the latter form is correct. *Nick's and Annie's cars were both vandalised in the same week.*

- Plurals of acronyms. An acronym is a 'word' made out of an abbreviation of two or more pre-existing words, such as CD for compact disc. Its plural is CDs, not CD's. Of course, you should write CD's if you mean a possessive (*My Blur CD's cover is missing*) or a contraction (*That CD's got a scratch on it*).

- Plurals of abbreviations. 'Ad' is short for advertisement, but it's still a word, and its plural is *ads*, not *ad's*. As with CD, the standard rule applies: *ad's* is correct for possessives or contractions. So:

> *The ads will all be ready by Tuesday.*

> *This ad's dreadful!*

> *She tried changing the ad's heading, but ended up revising the entire copy.*

- Eras written numerically. *The 60s* or *the 60's*? The former is correct, and will not be mistaken for a possessive. If you are going to use a possessive, much better to write out the word: *The sixties' gift to history was immense.* (Yes, I'm an old hippie at heart.)

That's probably enough on apostrophes. Just say one more time with me, please: 'I promise never to use *apostrophe-s* in a plural.'

Question marks are needed in direct speech but not in indirect (reported) speech.

> *He asked, 'Which route is for London?'*

But

> *He asked which route was for London.*

Exclamation marks are easy to overdo, especially when you are trying to sound informal. (They get used a lot in emails.) My advice is to write the piece and put in exclamation marks wherever you feel like so doing, then take out all of them, or all but the most important one, when you revise.

Of course, avoid multiple exclamation marks, except for comic effect!!!

The **dash** is informal, more like conversation. It's snappy – and probably overused. Rather than:

> *Fred Boggs – he played on the wing for Leicester City in the 1960s – now runs a pub in Kettering.*

just write:

> *Fred Boggs, who played on the wing for Leicester City in the 1960s, now runs a pub in Kettering.*

Note its use at the beginning of this paragraph (*It's snappy – and probably overused*). The dash often heralds bathos, a jokey change of direction of a sentence:

> *The volunteers were ready, willing – and totally incompetent.*

Bathos can also be used to more serious effect:

> *All the main political parties express concern about environmental issues – and do nothing about them when in office.*

The dash is often used when writing down speech.

> *I've just come in from the main office – it's bedlam
> there – those new people haven't a bloody clue – I've
> had several furious customers on the phone – items
> have been delivered to the wrong places* (etc.)

As with exclamation marks, I tend to overuse dashes in a first draft, then edit them out, replacing them with commas or colons.

The **hyphen** is used to make new words by joining existing ones. Examples abound (user-friendly, fast-moving, extra-special – apparently the most common one is long-term). There's a tendency for hyphens to vanish over time: when I was young, the local town had a by-pass built round it. Recently that has become so clogged that it's in need of a bypass.

Hyphens are useful in preventing confusion. One must assume that strict moralists approve of people having extra marital sex (as opposed to extra-marital sex), as that keeps married couples together and happy. But pity the doctor who arrived late one morning to find not thirty-odd but thirty odd people waiting for her surgery . . .

The three dots at the end of that last paragraph are called an **ellipsis**. The sense is of something more to be said, but left out because the reader either knows it already, or can guess. It is sometimes over-used in literary writing, to sound profound – which it can do, the first few times the author uses it.

Inverted commas are used for speech, and also as a gentle way of bracketing words.

For speech, get the positioning of the other punctuation right!

"Right," said Fred.

Fred said, "Right."

"Right," said Fred, "then left by the church, then right again." (Fred said one sentence, "Right, then left by the church . . .")

"Right," said Fred. "Let's go." (Fred said two sentences. "Right. Let's go.")

Don't forget that each new speaker starts a new paragraph.

"Right," said Fred.

"No, it's left," Mabel replied.

"It's right. I know; I've done this journey hundreds of times."

"You always have to be right about everything, don't you?"

Note that we don't need to say who spoke the third and fourth lines, as it's obvious. This is very useful, as it means we can miss out endless 'he saids' and 'she saids', and don't have to scrape around for increasingly bizarre synonyms.

Skilful writers also let us know who is speaking by signalling.

Fred scratched his head. "Hell, maybe it was left after all."

It's a matter of choice whether you use single or double inverted commas; just make sure you're consistent.

Single inverted commas are also used for what I call 'gentle bracketing'. This is a rather subtle use. Why did I use it just then? The immediate answer is because it felt right, but why did it feel right? Answer, I think, is that it's a kind of shorthand for saying 'the concept I refer to as the gentle bracket'. I'm signalling that it's a slightly odd phrase; I'm telling the reader not to waste time imagining floppy shelf supports and just accept 'gentle bracket' as a metaphor.

Single inverted commas are also used when the writer is being sarcastic:

> *The Government's current 'foreign policy'*

or when using a set or foreign phrase:

> *Great-Aunt Ethel believed strongly in the concept of 'noblesse oblige'.*

Lastly, some comments about capitals, underlines and italics. Are these strictly punctuation? Probably not, but I'm not sure where else to put them.

The rules governing **capitals** are rather complex. Clearly some aspects are easy – you begin sentences with capitals, form acronyms like CD from them, and put them at the start of place names and personal names. It starts getting complex with titles. The rule is 'capitalise when being specific, but not when being general'. So we visit Doctor Smith, but we don't go to see the Doctor, just the doctor. We say Amelia Jones is Managing Director of Associated Perfumes, but that most company managing directors earn over £100,000 a year. Even more elevated than the managing director, we pray to God, but say that polytheists worship many gods.

There's a tendency for bad writers to overuse capitals in the attempt to look important.

I have held several Marketing posts, especially Consumer Goods, and have worked on large Market Research Projects and an extended Customer Follow-up Survey . . .

The fact that the customer follow-up survey was a particular survey does not entitle it capitals, any more than Next-Door's Cat is entitled to capitals by being a particular cat. It is not a formal title. Such writing soon looks pompous and showy. This can, of course, be used for comic effect:

Julie's next Great Romance lasted at least a week.

Using capitals to highlight whole words is very crass, and should be reserved for people who write long, insulting emails to celebrities.

Italics, on the other hand, are a nice, tasteful way of highlighting something. Something *really* important. **Underlining** is a bit more brutal. Overuse of either waters them down.

Titles of books or films are often written in italics. In the past they might have been included in inverted commas, but this practice is anachronistic. Oddly, music doesn't seem to be treated in this way. We sit listening to Beethoven's Pastoral Symphony, reading *War and Peace* (if we're very cultured).

As well as using italics for emphasis, I use them in this book for examples, to ensure they stand out from the actual text. When I wrote crime fiction, there was a fashion for telling most of the story in one voice, with occasional buttings-in by another voice, often that of a psychopath. These were always in italics.

That's enough punctuation. If you want to go into it in greater depth, do go and buy Lynne Truss's book, or, if you don't want to follow the herd, a book called *Mind the Stop* by G.V. Carey.

As you get better at writing, you will enjoy using punctuation more and more. You'll start noticing how good writers use the 'big four' to help them pace their communication with their readers. You will experiment with punctuation in your own work, putting a comma somewhere, pondering the effect, taking it out again . . . Finally, you will understand why professional writers, when they're not talking about royalty payments or NUJ rates, often get into long discussions about semicolons and are clearly deliriously happy doing so.

Punctuation basics

- It's not a test – punctuation is there to help you help the reader.
- Remember the big four, and their relative 'pause values':
    Comma – 1 unit
    Semicolon – 2 units
    Colon – 2 ½ units
    Full stop – 4 units
- Get *its* and *it's* right!
- Avoid CAPITALS and lots of exclamation marks!!!

3 Grammatical errors

'Grammar' is basically the rules that make language work. Just as it's a marvel how we evolved our complex biological systems, it's a miracle how we evolved grammar. Our ancestors went around saying 'Ug'; now we speak these incredibly complex languages. In between, nobody sat down and designed language – like Topsy, it 'just growed'. Later on, people called grammarians took language to bits to see how it worked, just as doctors dissected bodies. The rules turned out to be very subtle and complicated, so much so that huge tomes are written on the intricacies. I don't want to go down that route, and would rather approach the subject by looking at common grammatical mistakes or quandaries.

Verbs not agreeing with subjects

The rule is simple: the verb 'agrees with' the subject.

- Singular subject, singular verb: *The cat sits on the mat.*

- Plural subject, plural verb: *The cats sit on the mat.*

- Two singular subjects, plural verb: *The cat and the dog sit on the mat.*

Easy!

But English being English, there's nothing totally easy. Of course there are 'irregular' verbs like *to be* (*I am sitting on the mat, you are sitting* etc.). But our verbs are a lot simpler than those of most other languages, so shouldn't cause too much misery. No, trickiness comes in with specific types of subject. 'Collective' nouns, for example – singular nouns that mean a group of individual beings or items. *The team **is** working on it* or *the team **are** working on it?*

Technically A is right, but B has become acceptable, as what is really being said is *(The people in) the team are working on it.*

Company names suffer from the same problem. Technically, they are singular. *Microsoft is one of the largest companies in the world.* But sometimes, when the massiveness or many-facetedness of the company is being highlighted, writers drift into the plural. *Microsoft are trying to get involved in every aspect of computing.* Personally, I'd stick to the singular.

So what about sports clubs? *Chelsea **are** top of the league* or *Chelsea **is** top of the league?* Oddly, the former, plural version sounds better (neither sounds good if you support a rival team), so I recommend using it. Yes, this is different from my advice on corporates. Perhaps this is because Chelsea are clearly a team – fans have pictures of them on their walls – while Microsoft is a company, a legal entity. (My 'inner nerd' has just objected that sports clubs can also be companies. So? Stick to the rule. *Manchester United has been bought by Malcolm Glazer.* This refers to the legal entity that owns and controls the team. *Manchester United are coming to Ewood Park in January.* Team: eleven chaps in red shirts.)

Double subjects can cause difficulties. *Jenny and I are going shopping* is easy: there are two of us, so the verb is plural. (Yes, some people even mess that up by saying *Jenny and me are going shopping . . .*) But what if it's just one of us, *Jenny <u>or</u> I . . .* ? *Jenny or I am going shopping* sounds odd but is actually technically correct, because the rule is that the verb agrees with the nearest subject.

My advice here is to walk away from the problem and rephrase, saying something like *Either Jenny is going shopping or I am*. Rephrasing is an important tool in the writer's armoury. It's often the best way out of impasses like this one, where all options sound or feel a bit odd; but some people feel afraid to rephrase, feeling that having produced a set of words, that's the only way of saying what needs to be said. English is wonderfully versatile, and there will always be other ways of getting your message across.

When subjects and complements are different numbers, the basic 'agreement' rule remains: the verb agrees with the subject.

> *Computer games **are** his only interest.*

> *His only interest **is** computer games.*

It may seem odd that the verb differs in 'number' in two sentences that convey exactly the same information – but that's how it is.

Remember that none, either, neither (and all other 'indefinite pronouns') are singular.

> *None of us **has** the answer.*

> *Neither of us **has** the answer.*

Split infinitives (*To boldly go . . .*)

These are an invention of pedantic eighteenth-century grammarians, who said that because Latin doesn't allow split infinitives, English shouldn't. But why shouldn't we use them in twenty-first-century Britain?

The answer is we shouldn't when it creates too much space between the *to* and the infinitive.

> *He began to slowly but surely turn the company round.*

sounds clumsy. Change the order:

> *He began to turn the company round, slowly but surely.*

Or, more 'flowery':

> *Slowly but surely, he began to turn the company round.*

In practice, it's best to avoid split infinitives, as some people think they are plain wrong.

Dangling participles

I love these. They add a welcome dash of surreal comedy to bad writing. I mean sentences like:

> *Suspended from a beam over the stage, the vicar switched on the village hall's new disco ball.*
>
> *Cycling along a path used by Dr Livingstone, a leopard leapt out and attacked me.*

It was the *new disco ball* that was actually *suspended from the beam*, and *I* who was *cycling along the path* – but that's not what the examples above say. Instead they sweep us away to a magical world of acrobatic vicars and leopards pedalling furiously on bikes. They do this because the rule is that the phrase at the beginning of the sentence, which contains a verb 'participle' (*suspended, cycling*), must refer to the *subject* of the main clause that follows (i.e. *the vicar, the leopard*). So the correct way of expressing the above gems would be:

> *Suspended from a beam over the stage, the village hall's new disco ball was switched on by the vicar.*

> *Cycling along a path used by Dr Livingstone, I was attacked by a leopard.*

Long may dangling participles continue to weave their magic! But let other people do the weaving, and don't fall into this trap yourself. Once you have sent your readers off on a wonderful surreal sidetrack, you'll have a job getting them back on the straight and narrow and taking you seriously.

Unbalanced sentences

If using 'correlative conjunctions' – which is the technical term for constructions like *either . . . or . . .* or *not only . . . but also . . .* – make sure each 'arm' of the expression bears the same weight and works correctly with the rest of the sentence.

For example:

> *We require students of either French or native speakers.*

should be

> *We require either students of French or native speakers.*

I'll talk more about balance in the section on style – but note that the above imbalance is not a style issue (which is about choosing options), but a grammatical one (the first example is incorrect).

'I' or 'me'?

> *Who's there?*
>
> *It's me.*

That's what people say, unless they're wearing capes and homburg hats, when they declaim, *It is I!*

Yet the cape-and-homburg brigade is technically correct. Back to parsing: *She likes me* is a standard subject-verb-object sentence. *She likes I* would be wrong as *me* is the correct 'object-form'. But *it is me* is a not a subject-verb-object sentence, but a subject-verb-*complement* sentence (remember – to be is a 'state'), for which *I* is correct.

That's fine, but we still don't say *It is I*; *It's me* has become standard, so you can use it in conversation, or in informal written communication like a quick email. But what about in more formal writing? Should you be incorrect or should you look pedantic? I think this is another impasse, to which the best response is to walk away and rephrase. For example:

> *It was me who suggested the rise in fees.*

should be

> *It was I who suggested . . .*

but can be rephrased as

> *I'm the person who suggested the rise in fees.*

This problem also surfaces with comparisons. *He is taller than me* is incorrect, but is what people say. *He is taller than I* is correct but sounds stilted. The simple way out is: *He is taller than I am.*

'Who' or 'whom'?

Whom is another technically correct word that's beginning to sound outdated. *To whom am I speaking?* is another cape-and-homburgism.

To get technical for a moment, you use *whom* if it refers to the object (direct or indirect) of the relative clause. So:

> *The man whom I mentioned yesterday.* (*The man* is the direct object of *mentioned*, the verb in the relative clause. I mentioned him.)

> *The man about whom I talked yesterday.* (*The man* is the indirect object of the verb in the relative clause. I talked about him.)

In spoken English, *whom* has pretty much disappeared – just say *the man I mentioned yesterday*, and everyone will understand. In written English this is becoming acceptable, but can be clumsy. My best advice is to try and avoid the sort of construction that would require a whom, but if you can't, then be correct. The worst thing is to say *the man who I mentioned yesterday*, which is both incorrect and easily avoidable.

Remember that *whom* is only used where it refers to the object of the relative clause, so *the man who sold me the car* (*the man* is the subject of the relative clause: he sold the car to me) is, of course, both correct and natural-sounding.

'That' or 'which'?

The lorry that drove past the house yesterday was red.

The lorry which drove past the house yesterday was red.

Is one right and one wrong? Do they mean exactly the same thing, or different things?

Answering the first question, the first sentence is correct; the second sentence will be correct when two commas have been inserted, so that it reads:

The lorry, which drove past the house yesterday, was red.

Answering the second question: the two sentences have subtly different meanings.

If you said *The lorry that drove past the house yesterday was red*, people would know nothing about this lorry at the start of the sentence, but by the end would have learned two things – that it drove past the house yesterday, and that it was red.

If you said *The lorry, which drove past the house yesterday, was red*, people would be right to ask, 'What lorry?' The force of the 'which' and the commas is to tell the listeners that they should already know something about this lorry, and they are now being told some extra things.

You've probably had enough grammar by this point! I could go on about the subject for ever, but I think I have covered the main areas where people go wrong or have doubts.

Never forget that you can always rephrase your way out of a grammatical quandary.

4 Spelling, confused words and gender

This is a bit of a catch-all chapter. It will be our last stint at boot camp, after which we can move onwards and upwards to the fascinating world of style.

Spelling

Most people now work on computers with spellcheckers. This makes life easier – you no longer have to remember how many c's and m's there are in 'accommodation' – but it also makes bad spelling even less pardonable. 'Whoever wrote the mis-spelt document that has just landed on my desk couldn't even be bothered to use a simple computer function!' However:

- Don't forget that some mis-spellings slip past the spellchecker. If you type in:

  I was so glad to receive a letter form you (spot the mistake)

  the spellchecker just sees ten recognisable words and moves on. The grammar checker, those green wavy lines that have the impertinence to tell me my sentences are too long, doesn't seem to find a problem with this either.

- By the same token, spellcheckers can object to perfectly correct use. For example, it didn't like *mis-spelt* above, objecting to *mis*. But that's a perfectly acceptable way of writing the word (and, in my view, the best way, as it avoids the potential for readers seeing the word *misspelt* and splitting it miss-pelt. Even if readers only do this for a moment, they have been halted in their reading flow unnecessarily).

- Make sure your spellchecker is set to US or UK English, depending on your readership.

There are some areas that your spellchecker will not help you with . . .

−ise and −ize

Should you write *organize* or *organise*? *Advertize* or *advertise*? *Magnetize* or *magnetise*?

The answer is that it depends. Some verbs absolutely require *–ise*. Others should technically be *–ize* but can be either. And there are some in the middle. But the rules are not all clear – even the great English usage gurus Fowler and Sir Ernest Gowers disagree on this topic.

Some verbs have to end in *–ise*. First, of course, verbs like *practise* that don't end in the 'ize' sound. But there are others – Fowler gives a list that includes *advertise, advise, apprise, chastise, circumcise, comprise, compromise, despise, devise, enfranchise, excise, exercise, improvise, revise, supervise, surmise* and *surprise*. From the other end, *–ize* is correct when existing nouns or adjectives have been converted into verbs by adding a suffix (the Ancient Greeks started it, with the suffix *–izein*) with the sense of 'to make something x'. Hence:

The Emperor Qin Shihuang standardized weights and measures throughout China

i.e. he made them standard. None of the '–ise only' verbs in the list above fits this model – you don't make something rev by revising it or make somebody surpr by surprising them.

Other words, like *organize/organise*, occupy the middle ground. Here, it is a matter of personal choice. In America, *–ize* is preferred. In the UK, the trend is towards using *–ise*. *Organize* is actually the original form (mediaeval Latin, *organizare*, since you ask), but it's best to stick to the convention of the audience for whom you are writing.

Licence, license, practise, practice

C is the noun, *s* the verb.

> *Sadly it was not the vicar's practice to practise what he preached.*
>
> *'Licensed premises' have been granted a licence to sell alcohol.*

I can't think of a way of remembering this, other than the rather lame mnemonic that the sea is a noun.

Enquiry, inquiry

An *inquiry* is a formal procedure, often set up to whitewash official incompetence or mendacity. An *enquiry* is simply a question. The verb is *to enquire* – but why not just use the word *ask*?

Effect, affect

The noun is now always *effect* (though there was once a noun *affect*, which meant an emotion). The verb is usually *to affect*. To *affect* means either 'to put something on for show' (*he affected a French accent*) or 'to have an effect on' (*rain affected his moods*). There's also a not hugely common verb *to effect*, meaning 'to bring something about' (*they effected an amazing turnaround at Megacorp*).

Principal, principle

Principal is an adjective meaning 'most important'; a *principle* is a moral belief. A principal is the head of an institution.

> *The college principal's principal principle was that of justice.*

Stationary, stationery

Stationary is the adjective (standing still); *stationery* the noun (pens, paper etc.).

Dependant, dependent

Just in case you thought the above constituted some kind of rule, here, the 'a' is the noun and the 'e' is the adjective.

> *Fred's dependants were dependent on him.*

Counsel, council

Counsel is advice (and the verb *to counsel*, to advise). You go to a counsellor for therapy.

Councils are legislative bodies, peopled by councillors.

Complement, compliment

A *complement* is a 'full amount', as in:

> *The regiment set off for battle with its complement of men.*

(This often appears as the tautology 'full complement'.)
    As a verb, *complement* usually means 'goes well with':

> *His boater complemented his striped blazer and MCC tie.*

Compliments are nice things people say.

Ordinance, ordnance

These are not hugely common words, but I have to admit I didn't actually know the difference before researching this book. An *ordinance* is a command; *ordnance* means military material, guns etc. The maps that walkers use are Ordnance Survey, which betrays their military origins. I'd been calling them 'Ordinance Survey' for years . . .

Aural, oral

Aural is to do with ears; *oral* with mouths. Life is made harder by the strange phrase *verbal agreement*, which really should be an *oral agreement*, as it is used to mean a spoken not a written agreement.

Confused words

The pairs of words above are **homophones**, which means they sound the same. Actually there are loads of these in English, but the ones I've listed above are the ones that cause most confusion when spelling. Other homophones include *formerly* and *formally*, *idol* and *idle*, *prince* and *prints*, *presence* and *presents*, *Wales*, *wails* and *whales* – but I rarely see these mistaken. *Pray silence for His Highness the Prints of Whales.*

A related topic is that of words that sound almost the same *but not quite*, and which get confused and/or misused. I mean words like:

Enormousness and enormity

This particularly irritates me, as a powerful word is being neutered by misuse. Yes, I know language is perpetually changing, and I relish that fact, especially when evocative and fun new words like *bling* come into use. But here the change is for the worse. For those of you who don't know, an *enormity* is a particularly evil human action, or set of human actions, such as the Holocaust or Stalin's Gulags. *Enormousness* just means 'bigness'. So why do intelligent people who should know better talk about *the enormity of the task in preparing for the Olympics*?

Mitigate and militate

Mitigating circumstances are those which lessen the responsibility someone has for a crime (or in some sense make it more understandable). To *militate* is to have an effect, as in:

> *The recent scandals have not militated against the president's popularity.*

I often hear a sentence like:

> *The recent scandals have not mitigated against the president's popularity.*

This is, of course, gibberish.

Imply and infer

To *imply* is to make a hint; to *infer* is to take a hint. Sometimes infer is used wrongly for imply. *The PM inferred in her speech that a cabinet reshuffle was imminent.* No, she implied it; we did the inferring.

Consist, comprise and constitute

Comprise is the slippery one here. *To consist of* simply means 'to be made up of' in the sense of *the team consists of eleven players. To constitute* simply means 'to make up' in the sense of *eleven players constitute a cricket team.*

Comprise used just to mean the same as 'consist of' but slithered across the semantic floor many years ago to mean 'constitute' as well. So one can say *The USA comprises 50 states* and *The 50 states comprise the USA.* Recently the word has done more slithering, and people say things like *The USA is comprised of 50 states.* This is just plain wrong. Arguably we'd be best off not using comprise at all. If you are in the position to choose between a word that has one, clear, generally understood meaning, and a word with lots of meanings, go for the first option every time.

Prescribe, proscribe

These are virtual opposites, yet people often mix them up. Your doctor *prescribes* medicine, but *proscribes* smoking and drinking (though most of the doctors I know seem to enjoy the odd drink or four . . .).

As with *comprise*, it's probably best to avoid *proscribe*, and just use a synonym like *forbid* – that way there'll be no misunderstandings.

Continuous, continual

Continuous means unending; *continual* means very frequent. Not even the most annoying person in the world complains continuously, which would mean whinging 24 hours a day, seven days a week, without drawing breath (actually, I think I have worked with a couple of people like that). Some people do, however, complain continually, i.e. often.

Flaunt and flout

To *flaunt* something is to show it off, in a crude and excessive way. Peacocks flaunt their tails. To *flout* is to ignore a rule, deliberately and slightly provocatively – *the teenager flouted the no-smoking signs and lit a cigarette.* Flaunt is perhaps a stronger word than flout, and I guess that's why people use it wrongly, thinking that flaunting a rule is breaking it in an even more assertive way than flouting it. It isn't, of course.

Anyone who likes using language with precision – and to write clearly and elegantly, you should use language with precision – will enjoy finding more words that get mangled together in poor usage and prising them apart. I have a *Dictionary of Confusable Words* which it is fun, and useful, to browse through at odd moments.

Often I find I've been getting things wrong for years, as in those 'Ordinance Survey' maps. And I'm supposed to be a professional . . .

The gender trap

This isn't something MI5 warns its agents about, but a danger to writers – that they will alienate half their readership by talking about *he, him* or *his* all the time (or about *she, her* and *hers* all the time, but this is much less common).

The problem is that this isn't just about being watchful for gender bias. There are various ways round this bias, but all of them create problems. (If there were an ideal solution, we'd all be using it now as a matter or course, and this section would be much shorter.)

Imagine we have a sentence from a 1970s book on driving. *The driver must put on his seatbelt before starting his car.* How do we remove the gender bias from that?

Go plural

This is often the easiest solution.

> *Drivers must put on their seatbelts before starting their cars.*

It does, however, create a slightly different, and more distant, mental image. Instead of a person getting into a car (that's me!), there are lots of people getting into lots of cars.

Address the reader directly

This works well in some situations. If this is an instruction manual, just say:

> *Put on your seatbelt before starting your car.*

Of course, if this were an objective description of a process *(Since 197X, the law in the UK has stated that the driver must put on . . .)*, this wouldn't work, but if the sentence were part of such an objective description, it would matter less if the writing were 'more distant', so option 1 above *(drivers must put on . . .)* would be fine.

Substitute an article

In other words:

> *The driver must put on the seatbelt before starting the car.*

This sounds a little colder than the original, however, and might not suit the mood the author is trying to create. (It's *my* seatbelt, and *my* car!)

Say *he or she* or *she or he*

Used sparingly, this works well. The trouble is that it can become ugly and silly quite quickly.

> *The driver must put on his or her seatbelt before starting his or her car. He or she must do this every time he or she gets his or her car out of the garage, even if he*

*or she is only going to the local shop or picking up his or
her child from school.*

Use the 'singular they'

The 'singular they' is common after indefinite pronouns – such as
anyone, *each* – which are technically followed by singular verbs:

Each to their own

or following *each* as an adjective:

We encourage each child to fulfil their potential.

Despite the bleatings of grammarians, this principle has been
followed by Shakespeare, Dr Johnson, Lord Byron and Sir Winston
Churchill. If it's good enough for them, it's good enough for me.

The 'singular they' is becoming more and more used in other
situations as well:

*The driver must put on their seatbelt before starting
their car.*

Two riders:

First, you must be sure that it is totally clear what *they* or *their*
refer to. In the example above there is no problem with this – *their*
clearly refers to *the driver* – but in another context, havoc could
ensue. (I talk more about this in the section on 'wandering
pronouns' – see p. 53.)

Second, this new usage may alienate some purist readers.

Alternate

Some writers get round the problem by alternating. They talk about *his* for a while, then *hers*. Make sure, however, that you don't mysteriously change the sex of a protagonist. If I read *The driver should put on his seatbelt*, I form an image in my mind of a male driver. I find it odd if in the next chapter the driver is female. This isn't male chauvinism – I'd be just as nonplussed if I was told in the first chapter that the driver was female, and found her in the next one to be male.

The truth is that there is no magical way out of the gender trap. The best solution is to have all the above weapons in your armoury, and to deploy them appropriately and intelligently.

5 Style – 'flow' and its enemies

The last four chapters have been largely about rules. Having taken these on board, it's time to look at style – how to write English that is not just free of mistakes (the right place to start), but which is actively elegant, attractive and effective. This is more about choice, skill and – something we should all aspire to – artistry.

As I write, I can hear a particular kind of macho boss saying, 'Don't give me all this "style" crap, just get it right and tell me the facts!'

But, of course, things aren't that simple. Writing that is grammatically correct can still fail to deliver information because it is unclear or boring. Think back to when you were last faced by a piece of managementese, and remember that sense of switching off that came over you after a few lines.

> *In this presentation a number of initiatives are subjected to an examination process with respect to viability and ongoing strategic relevance . . .*

Look what happens:

In this presentation . . . A fair start, though what I am reading is a document, not a presentation.

a number of initiatives . . . Hmm. 'A number of . . .' is vague, and 'initiatives' is a buzzword that can mean anything.

are subjected to an examination process . . . Things are looking bad. I assume the writer means *the initiatives are examined*, but instead we've got this over-elaborate form of words. Experience is beginning to tell me this is going to be hard work, and I'm already beginning to switch off. However, I keep trying.

with respect to viability . . . More empty words.

and ongoing strategic relevance . . . Oh, God.

It's a fact, used by hypnotists and NLP therapists, that poor English sends people into a kind of hypnotic trance. The act of reading carries on, but the act of *understanding*, whereby you extract information from what you read and transfer it deeper into the brain, has stopped. Hence that experience we've all had, of putting down a badly written report and realising that we've been scanning it for ten minutes and haven't actually taken in a single thing.

There is, however, a flip-side to the trance. There is 'good trance', too. People actively enjoy reading interesting material. Curiosity is one of our most basic animal instincts, and our brains have the capacity to get into what psychologists call a 'flow' state. You are reading. Your brain is busy processing the information from that reading, not just skimming but busily filing it away into deep levels of memory and understanding. And it feels nice – you're involved and happy. (There's a fascinating book on this 'flow' state, by psychologist Mihaly Csikszentmihalyi – lecturers tend to refer to him as Mihaly – which I recommend.)

Good writing is all about getting your readers into this state, and keeping them there. The Golden Rule to achieve this is: *Every word should lead your reader forward.*

I mean that. Every word should make things clearer to the reader, or give them new information, or in some way help them along the journey that is comprehending the piece you have written.

Let's look at the Golden Rule itself:

- *Every*. This sets up certain expectations in the reader: some kind of generalisation follows. Every what?

- *Word*. Now we know. Actually, I would like to say more than 'word'. Every punctuation mark should be leading your reader forward, too. But let's keep things simple.

- *Should*. Obviously this shows that I'm laying down the law here. But there exists a range of 'obligation' words: why have I chosen 'should' rather than 'must' or 'ought'? The answer is realism. 'Must' implies failure if an instruction is not carried out to the letter. 'Should' implies an obligation, but not such an iron one as 'must': perfection isn't attainable; just do the best you can . . .

- *Lead*. The main verb in a sentence is often the most powerful word in that sentence, so choose a verb that is as clear and specific as possible. When I first formulated this maxim, I used the word 'move' rather than 'lead', but it felt too general and too weak. Leading implies so much more: there's a direction you are going in; you, the writer, know this direction; you're heading there yourself; you are going to take the reader with you. Good writing is leadership.

- *Your*. Again, when I first formulated this maxim, I said 'the reader'. But 'the' is too remote, too general. To say *your* reader makes the additional point that readers have a relationship with you. They are taking time out of their busy life to attend to you.

- *Reader*. The object of the sentence, another key word.

- *Forward*. In a sense this is not a powerful word, as it is partially implied by *lead*; but not totally. Bad writers lead their readers round and round in circles or into quagmires. You will lead your readers *forward*, towards goals you clearly understand.

Before you start a piece, you must have a clear idea of what you want your readers to know; and when you call a piece 'finished', you must have a strong conviction that the piece conveys this knowledge. In practice, the process is a little more complex: as you write you often become aware of new things – new subtleties; old certainties that suddenly don't look so certain; new certainties. These become the new 'must-says'. (Arthur Miller said that he often started a play unsure of what it was really about, but at some point he realised what the basic theme was, at which point he wrote it on a piece of paper, stuck that to his typewriter, and built the play around it.) The end result, whether you start out knowing exactly what you want to say, or whether you work out what you want to say as you write, must be the same: clear direction, clear messages, the reader left in no doubt.

A lot went into the choice of those seven words. Seven words that we, as bright, literate adults, read in a moment; but don't be fooled by the quickness of our reading into underrating the brilliance of the brain. In that moment, it will carry out the complex tasks of taking in not only the words but also the many subtleties of meaning that come with them. As writers we must live with this fact – that our work is going to be subjected to a precise, intense, subconscious scrutiny. But we can also enjoy the 'upside' – that if our words pass this scrutiny, the reader's brain will both rejoice and get to work on the content.

All the chapters on style in this book are ultimately about this 'flow' state: how to maintain it and how to lose it. For the rest of this chapter I shall look at the three most common and damaging flow-stoppers: ambiguity, repetition and jargon.

Ambiguity

At best, ambiguity is comical:

> *We're delighted to announce the appointment of John Soames as church organist. We couldn't get a better man!*

At worst, it leaves the reader puzzled: the opposite of what you want, which, remember, is to lead your reader forward.

Most courses on writing teach 'avoid ambiguity' – and they are right to do so; but this is too weak a formulation. Ambiguity isn't something nasty that one can take a step or two to avoid, but a cancer at the soul of good communication that must be battled with all the weapons at the writer's disposal. I prefer to say, *Seek out, and eliminate, all ambiguity, actual or potential.*

The most powerful tool for battling ambiguity is the ability to stand back from what you have just written and see it from the reader's viewpoint. The magic question is not, 'Does this say what I want it to?' but something much stronger. 'Is there any way that an intended reader could look at this and interpret it in any other way other than the way I intend them to?' If the answer is, 'Yes, well, maybe . . .' then get rewriting.

A major cause of ambiguity is **wandering pronouns**. Every time you use a *he, she, it* or *they*, or a *this* or a *that*, you must ask yourself: 'Does the reader *unambiguously* know what that pronoun refers to?' If there's the slightest doubt, rewrite.

> *Charles came into the room and sat next to Henry. He was very unhappy.*

Who was unhappy? Probably Charles, as he is the subject of the first sentence, but some readers might see the *Henry* right next to the *he*, and draw the opposite conclusion. This is not good enough, and the skilled writer will rephrase this.

Here are Charles and Henry again:

> *Henry sat in the old chair. Charles came in and sat next to him. He was very unhappy.*

Again, this should be clear. A common-sense rule is that in any paragraph, we establish early on who or what the paragraph is about, and that all appropriate pronouns and possessives then apply to this person or thing for the rest of the paragraph. Here this has been done: we open the paragraph with Henry, and use *him* in the next sentence to cement the point. The reader should now think, 'For the rest of this paragraph, if I see a *he* or a *him*, I know that refers to Henry.'

The trouble is that reading just isn't that simple. In some way, by beginning the next sentence with Charles, the writer has moved the focus from Henry to Charles, and so the reader is left with a whisper of ambiguity. 'It's probably Henry who is unhappy, but it just might be Charles.' Such whispers of ambiguity are enough to break the reader's flow, so must be avoided.

In the paragraph above, I originally wrote:

> *In some way, by beginning the next sentence with Charles, the writer has moved the focus to him . . .*

Technically, this was correct, but I still felt there was a possible doubt about *him*. Yes, the pronoun probably refers to Charles, but there are other males around in the paragraph – Henry, 'the writer', a male reader – so I ended up saying:

In some way, by beginning the next sentence with Charles, the writer has moved the focus from Henry to Charles . . .

Of course, this raises the spectre of repetition (see below), but it's always better to repeat a word than to use a pronoun whose antecedent is not 100 per cent clear to the reader.

It is particularly troublesome, because it is used in various ways:

- to refer to a single item (*This is an E22. It supersedes our old model.*)

- to refer to a process (*It never pays to take the M25 on Friday afternoons.*)

- to refer to a generality like the weather (*It's raining!*)

This can produce classic howlers like:

They were drinking cold beer because it was warm.

Switch on the ambiguity detectors, and rephrase.

It was such a lovely day that they got out the cold beers.

Watch out for *this* and *that*. An example:

In the light of the above comments, there are essentially three reactions to being invited to tender for a contract:

  1. To politely decline.

  2. To accept, and make an all-out effort to win the work.

  3. To accept, but just 'go through the motions'.

This may sound strange, but if pursued consciously and
deliberately does have a purpose.

What does *this* refer to? Technically, *this* refers to the most recent item mentioned, which, here, is the third reaction listed. But it could be misinterpreted as referring to everything that has gone before in the paragraph, to the whole business of having these three reactions. Rather than risk misdirecting the reader, be clear. In the example above, the technically correct use of *this* (reaction 3) is also the one intended – but readers don't want technical correctness, they want clarity. So rephrase:

The third of these reactions may sound strange . . .

Note that **possessives** (*my*, *yours*, *hers* etc.) can go wandering too:

The foreman was angry because Fred landed on his
head.

Whose head? As with wandering pronouns, the best way out is to rephrase:

The foreman was angry because Fred fell and suffered
head injuries.

Watch out also for **other wanderers** like *only*, *almost*, *even*. These must go right in front of the word or phrase they are qualifying, or you will not say what you mean. Here is *only* making its way through a simple sentence, qualifying different words or phrases (highlighted in **bold** type), and implying totally different things each time:

*Only **we** sent him to the shop to buy tomatoes.*
(Everyone else made him stay at home.)

*We only **sent** him to the shop to buy tomatoes.* (We
didn't stick a gun in his back and scream 'Go!')

*We sent only **him** to the shop to buy tomatoes.* (But half
the class went with him, too.)

*We sent him only **to the shop** to buy tomatoes.*
(Because the tomatoes on sale at other outlets are
rubbish.)

*We sent him to the only **shop** to buy tomatoes.* (A clumsy
sentence, but not meaningless. It tells us that we sent
him to buy tomatoes, and, by the way, there's only one
shop in Xville, where we're staying at the moment.)

*We sent him to the shop only **to buy tomatoes**.* (But
while he was there he tried to get a job as an assistant
and asked the girl on the till for a date as well.)

*We sent him to the shop to only **buy** tomatoes.* (But he
ended up talking about tomatoes, comparing different
types of tomato and even offering to supply the shop
with some tomatoes he'd grown himself.)

*We sent him to the shop to buy only **tomatoes**.* (But
he came back with cabbages, eggs, potatoes and a
tin of beans.)

In practice, one can relax these rules a little if the context makes
the meaning obvious. For example, if you actually express the
implications:

> *We only sent him to the shop to buy tomatoes – but he ended up talking about tomatoes, comparing different types of tomato and even offering to supply the shop with some tomatoes he'd grown himself.*

The meaning is now perfectly clear.

When I rewrite, much of my effort goes into removing potential ambiguities, even the tiniest ones. If you consider this pernickety, remember that your aim is to get the reader into a state of 'flow'. If you break this flow with an ambiguity, even if the reader 'should have got what you meant', you have stopped communicating. If there is one area of writing where I do advocate zero tolerance, it is this one. Be ruthless with ambiguity.

Ambiguity in literature

In literary writing, ambiguity is often valued – at the most basic level, as puns (Shakespeare loved them), but also at a deeper level, as a way of showing that we operate from conflicting motives and that life itself is still, despite the efforts of scientists, sociologists, psychologists and all the other ologists, essentially complex, surprising, mysterious and resistant to analysis. Poet and critic William Empson even wrote a book praising the *Seven Types of Ambiguity* that writers could use to reinforce this point.

Good for him. In the kind of writing this book is about, don't use any type of ambiguity. It may be a complex and crazy world, but the good non-fiction writer's job is to create small islands of clarity in that world. Avoid ambiguity at all costs – no excuses!

Repetition

Unnecessary repetition breaks our Golden Rule that every word should lead your reader forward. Unnecessary repetition doesn't lead the reader anywhere – except towards that tipping point where their brain leaves a state of 'flow' and starts to go into a trance of boredom.

I say 'unnecessary repetition', because obviously some words have to be repeated, like *the* or key concepts or characters' names.

A hint – don't take too much notice of this advice when writing your first draft. Just get the words down. It's when rewriting that you should focus on removing repetitions. Here are the main ways of doing this:

1. Rephrase (usually the best way).

2. Simply leave out unnecessary repetitions.

3. Use pronouns – when you can do so with zero ambiguity.

4. Use a few synonyms.

5. Use 'the former' and 'the latter'.

In the example below, I use techniques 1, 2 and 4. Here's a 'first-draft' passage:

> *There are differences between mainland Chinese and overseas Chinese. The mainland Chinese tend to think of all Chinese including the overseas Chinese as part of the Chinese cultural family. The overseas Chinese are more aware of the political differences between mainland China and the countries of the Chinese diaspora, though they are aware that they share an*

underlying common cultural heritage with the
mainland Chinese.

Rewriting this, we get:

There are differences between mainland and overseas
Chinese (simple rephrasing). *The mainlanders* (another
simple rephrase: we have established that we are
talking about Chinese) *tend to think of all Chinese* (fine
to restate 'Chinese' here – don't be too afraid of
repetition and wander off into flights of fancy like
'sons and daughters of the Middle Kingdom'),
wherever they are in the world, (another rephrase) *as*
part of one (it's obviously Chinese) *cultural family.*
Overseas Chinese (again, fine to restate 'Chinese',
especially as 'overseas Chinese' is pretty much a stock
phrase) *are more aware of the political contrasts*
(synonym, avoiding repetition of 'differences') *between*
mainland China and the countries of the diaspora
(obviously, from the context, the *Chinese* diaspora),
though they are aware that they share an underlying
(have left out 'common cultural', as that is another
unnecessary repetition: if they share it, it is 'common';
and heritage is cultural, unless we're being very specific
and talking about Aunt Ethel's will) *heritage.*

Or, without the comments:

There are differences between mainland and overseas
Chinese. The mainlanders tend to think of all Chinese,
wherever they are in the world, as part of one cultural
family. Overseas Chinese are more aware of the

political contrasts between mainland China and the
countries of the diaspora, though they are aware that
they share an underlying heritage.

Rewriting is not always just a one-step process. Looking at the above, there is still more that could be done to improve it. For example, we could leave out the last clause, as we have already been told that mainlanders see all Chinese as *part of one cultural family*:

There are differences between mainland and overseas
Chinese. The mainlanders tend to think of all Chinese,
wherever they are in the world, as part of one cultural
family. Overseas Chinese are more aware of the
political contrasts between mainland China and the
countries of the diaspora.

And if we aren't 100 per cent sure that readers will understand the term *diaspora*, that could be simplified to:

There are differences between mainland and overseas
Chinese. The mainlanders tend to think of all Chinese,
wherever they are in the world, as part of one cultural
family. Overseas Chinese are more aware of the
political contrasts between mainland China and their
adopted countries.

And why not tighten up the distinction at the heart of the passage by explaining:

There are differences between mainland and overseas
Chinese. The mainlanders tend to think of all Chinese,
wherever they are in the world, as part of one cultural

family. Overseas Chinese are more aware of the political contrasts between mainland China and their adopted countries, and of the cultural effects of those contrasts over the last sixty years.

(Note that the repetition of *contrasts* is fine, as it is doing a job – tying culture and politics together, which is the key point the passage is making.)

The paragraph is not yet perfect, as it begins by saying *there are differences*, yet actually just describes one difference – so more work needed, but let's move on!

In the next example, we see where an author has taken to heart the advice to avoid repetition, but gone overboard on technique 4, using synonyms.

Everton started well, but were soon under pressure. Jones rattled the Liverpool club's crossbar in the 23rd minute, and Manchester City scored on the half-hour with a header from Smith. However, as the half drew to an end, the Toffees began to fight back, and on 43 minutes the Goodison-Park-based team finally scored from a set piece. The men in blue went into half-time in good spirits.

This is, I suppose, better than:

Everton started well, but were soon under pressure. Jones rattled the Everton crossbar in the 23rd minute, and Manchester City scored on the half-hour with a header from Smith. However, as the half drew to an end, Everton began to fight back, and on 43 minutes Everton finally scored from a set piece. Everton went into half-time in good sprits.

But miles better is:

> *Everton started well, but were soon under pressure.*
> *Jones rattled their* (it's perfectly clear who 'their' refers
> to, as no other club has been mentioned) *crossbar in*
> *the 23rd minute, and Manchester City scored on the*
> *half-hour with a header from Smith. However, as the*
> *half drew to an end, Everton* (it's reasonable to use the
> club name again here, especially as by doing so we set
> them up as the obvious antecedent for pronouns in
> the rest of the paragraph) *began to fight back, and on*
> *43 minutes they* (obviously Everton) *finally scored*
> *from a set piece. They* (I think it's still quite clear who
> 'they' refers to, but if you wanted to use a synonym
> here, that would also be fine. Of the synonyms on offer,
> 'the men in blue' is by far the most vivid, bringing to
> mind a picture of men leaving a football field, so use
> that one – though, of course, you will then have three
> 'in's in the last sentence, so would need to do some
> rephrasing) *went into half-time in good sprits.*

Or, without my explanations . . .

> *Everton started well, but were soon under pressure.*
> *Jones rattled their crossbar in the 23rd minute, and*
> *Manchester City scored on the half-hour with a header*
> *from Smith. However, as the half drew to an end,*
> *Everton began to fight back, and on 43 minutes finally*
> *scored from a set piece. Half-time found the men in*
> *blue in good sprits.*

Technique 5, 'the former' and 'the latter', is beginning to sound a bit outdated, but it is still useful, so keep using it unless you're writing something very informal.

Technically, these words can be used only to distinguish between *two* alternatives.

> *We were offered spaghetti, macaroni and tagliatelle,*
> *and chose the latter*

is incorrect, though hardly a great sin, as most readers will get what you mean and it doesn't sound silly. But there's no sense in unnecessarily breaking rules: just say 'the last one'.

Much worse is to say:

> *Emma came into the room. The latter was full of*
> *children's toys.*

This is technically wrong because former and latter are about distinguishing between already stated alternatives, so the second sentence implies that Emma might have been full of children's toys, but, no, actually it was the room.

> *Emma looked into the kitchen and the sitting room.*
> *The latter was full of children's toys*

is of course correct, neat and good style.

> *Emma came into the room. The latter was full of*
> *children's toys*

can be rephrased a number of ways.

> *Emma came into the room. It was full of children's toys*

is simplest and thus best. But if, for some reason based on something earlier in the text, you feel that the pronoun 'it' might be ambiguous, then try:

> *Emma came into the room, which was full of children's toys.*

Note, however, that literary writing can use repetition successfully for effect (*Onward, onward rode the six hundred . . .*), as can political speech-writers:

> *. . . we shall fight in France, we shall fight on the seas and oceans, we shall fight with growing confidence and growing strength in the air, we shall defend our Island, whatever the cost may be; we shall fight on the beaches, we shall fight on the landing grounds, we shall fight in the fields and in the streets, we shall fight in the hills; we shall never surrender.*

Unlike ambiguity, which should always be avoided, repetition can be used as long as you do so knowingly, as part of your plan to keep leading your reader forward.

Jargon

There are two sorts of jargon, one much more pernicious than the other, but both impolite and destructive of reader 'flow'.

One type is the **inappropriate use of technical terms**.

There is nothing wrong with using technical terms when communicating exclusively with fellow technicians. Indeed, it's poor writing not to. Here are a few lines from a report on a cricket match:

Pietersen lofted Khan over mid-on twice in the over,
but, after a scrambled single from Panesar, found
himself facing Ahmed. He pushed forward to a googly
with uncharacteristic tentativeness and lobbed a bat-
pad chance to silly-mid-off, who snaffled it with ease.

Meaningless jargon? No, not if the report is in *Willow on Leather Quarterly*, whose cricket-buff readers will be perfectly familiar with terms like googly and silly mid-off, and actually would not understand the piece if these terms were not used. But if the piece were in *Cricket: A Guide for Beginners*, it would be jargon of the worst kind (unless, I suppose, it were being used as an example – *by the end of this book, you will actually be able to read this and understand every word!*)

In practice, you sometimes have to use technical terms when writing for non-technical people. You should do this apologetically: 'I'm sorry, I can't think of any other way of doing this . . .' The fault is yours for not being able to get round the problem, not your readers' for not being in the know.

Use the following techniques:

- Flag up that it's a technical term, so the reader doesn't feel stupid.

- Explain the term the first time you introduce it.

- Use diagrams or pictures. If it's computer-related, show what the user's screen will look like.

- Have a glossary at the end, so that when people forget what an xnogdothrope is – which they will do – they can look the term up rather than have to search back through the text for the first reference.

- Have an index, so that if people still want to find that first reference, they can do so.

The other form of jargon is what I call '**Dalek-speak**' – a name inspired by *Private Eye* magazine, which has a little section citing real-life examples of this stuff, with a picture of one of those evil, lumbering automata from the *Dr Who* TV programmes. I could have used other terms – managementese, corporate-speak, management bollocks, bullshit – but I like the image of the Daleks. Daleks don't speak, they intone, in a machine-like voice that is completely lacking in either thought or feeling.

Listen to the Radio 4 news in the morning, and you get excellent reports from professional journalists (or moving comments from the general public who are being interviewed). Then it's time for the business section: a CEO of some corporation comes on; suddenly the Daleks have landed . . .

> *We are prioritising our resource structure by initiating a strategic withdrawal procedure from customer-facing operations in order to concentrate on our core, web-based activities . . .*

It's important to understand that this isn't just inappropriate use of technical terms. It's worse than that. *Initiating* is not a technical term, but (in this case) a pompous, Dalek-way of saying 'beginning'. *Customer-facing operations* is a pompous, Dalek-way of saying 'shops'. There's a simple test. If you hear a strange word or phrase, can it be explained in intelligible English that is shorter? If so, then it is *not* a technical term, but Dalek-speak.

> *Customer-facing operations* versus 'shops'? *Dalek-speak.*

> *Silly-mid-off* versus 'a position where the fielder stands close to the batsman, at about 30 degrees to him and to his right'? *Technical term.*

This is not to say that management does not have any technical terms. Finance has plenty. Ask an accountant what 'accruals' means, and they'll go on all night.

Below are some Dalek terms, with their ordinary English translations.

DALEK-SPEAK	CLEAR ENGLISH
alleviate	lessen
concerning	about
documentation	documents, papers
due to the fact that	because
increment	pay rise
necessitate	require
ongoing	continuing
indebtedness	debt
utilise	use
purchase (verb)	buy
In the event of x	If x happens
currently	now (*or just leave out*)
avail oneself of	use
augment	increase
with respect to	about
initiate	begin
terminate	end
exterminate! exterminate!	Hello, nice to meet you

And so on . . .

Sadly, new Dalek words are always being created. The other day I was emailed a time and a date for a meeting, but the venue hadn't been *concretised*. No problem: a venue made of wood or brick would have been fine.

Even more sadly, there's more to Dalek-speak than just individual pompous, ugly, empty words. Our language itself gets messed around with. One of the curses of Dalek-speak is rampant 'nominalisation'. OK, that's a long word, but it's a technical term to describe the turning of words into nouns – in this case, strong, vivid verbs into dull nouns. For example:

> *apply* becomes *make an application*
>
> *evaluate* becomes *perform an evaluation of.*

This becomes even worse when the dull, nominalised noun is considered still too interesting, and becomes a kind of half-noun half-adjective, qualifying an even duller noun:

> *apply* now becomes *undergo an application procedure*
>
> *evaluate* now becomes *perform an evaluation process on.*

No doubt, if a management cat sat on a corporate mat, we would be told that:

> *The feline has actioned a mat-located sedentary procedure.*

Pointers to nominalisation include:

- Nouns ending in –ion.

- Dull verbs – *make, effect, action* or just *to be.*

- Words like *procedure, process.*

- A sudden desire to be doing anything other than reading this drab, soulless rubbish.

The solution is to get back to a verb that describes the actual act being performed. It's amazing how much more refreshing a piece becomes the moment this is carried out.

Why has Dalek-speak caught on? The obvious reason is conformity. If you join Megacorp, you have to learn to speak like this or you won't get ahead. This, of course, begs the question of why Megacorp has developed this culture. I've heard it said that Dalek-speak makes it easer for non-native English speakers to assimilate. I cannot believe this – is it really easier to learn to say *undergo an application procedure* rather than *apply*? Other people argue that Dalek-speak is a pure, intellectual language, with all surplus emotional content removed, and thus appropriate for the pure, intellectual activity that is business (academics use the same argument). It doesn't sound very intellectual to me – and even if it were, is business really just a purely cerebral activity? Academics have more excuse for desiring totally dry writing – but not when communicating with the general public. Academics also have a responsibility to their students, most of whom will not pursue careers in academia, to teach them not just buzz-words but the basics of clear, intelligent argument and expression.

I fear that, at least in part, the rise of Dalek-speak is about human nature. When I was about seven, I was in a gang where we had special code words. As a teenager, I joined a kind of giant gang called 'youth culture' that created all sorts of slang – most of it a lot more poetic and imaginative than Dalek-speak. Grown-ups and uncool fellow teenagers were not supposed to understand these words, and much humour was gained from their botched attempts to use them. I trust I have grown out of such attitudes and behaviour – which are, of course, based on insecurity. Proper grown-ups don't need to exclude others from their communication, or to look down on 'outsiders', do they . . . ?

I don't want to go on about this. Jargon is arrogant, not intellectual at all but lazy, and, worst of all from the point of view of this book, lousy communication. Avoid it.

In the next chapter, I shall present some rules for producing English that is the opposite of jargon: clear, accessible and powerful. I'd like to end this chapter with an experiment. Imagine a modern Winston Churchill, who instead of studying history and politics, read business studies, did an MBA and got an excellent job with Hypercorp . . .

> *We will initiate an ongoing conflict process in France; we will engage in combative behaviours in non-land locations of both small and non-small extent; we will instigate a belligerence situation, with incrementally rising levels of personnel morale and capacity to deliver, in the aerial environment. We shall activate defensive procedures with respect to our island, irrespective of cost constraints. Military engagement strategies will also be rolled out in the following locations:*
>
> * *Land/sea interfaces*
>
> * *Designated areas for transferring combat personnel from seaborne to land-based modality*
>
> * *Fields*
>
> * *Streets*
>
> * *Hills (not exceeding 500 metres in altitude).*
>
> *We are not currently anticipating finalising hostilities with a negative win outcome.*

Help! We've just lost the Second World War.

6 Style – making your writing lively

Having dealt with the big three enemies of clear, 'flow-inducing' writing, it's time to get more positive. Here are twelve ways to make your writing lively. Lively writing engages and pleases the reader. Lively writing sends readers into that 'good trance', the 'flow' state where they are both taking in information and enjoying the experience.

Use the active voice

I'm sure you know the difference.

> In *Boris hit Fred* the verb is in the active voice
>
> In *Fred was hit by Boris* the verb is in the passive voice

Lively writing uses the active voice. Of any scene, we ask three basic questions:

- Who's doing the action?

- What are they doing?

- To whom? (Or to what?)

These are, of course, the 'subject, verb, object' of parsing. I believe this is the natural way in which our brains take in information. This is true even in complex sentences, where we have to work harder to find these things, but still go hunting for them on first sight. To mess with this is to risk sacrificing the efficient transmission of information from page to recipient's understanding – the whole point of non-fiction writing.

Yet mess with it we do. The passive voice is used all the time in business and official writing.

> *It has been decided to refuse your application . . .*

> *A recommendation has been made by the inspectors that . . .*

Why? One reason is that some people believe there is a rule that says you shouldn't use *I* or *we* in formal communication. This may be true in certain kinds of academic essays, but even there I'm not convinced – a good academic piece should weigh facts and opinions as objectively as possible, but in the end, the reader wants an opinion from the writer, so why not be upfront and say *I* or *we*? It is certainly not true outside academia, where individuals, businesses and other organisations are trying to get a message across to other people effectively and quickly.

Sometimes, sadly, use of the passive is simply a screen to hide behind. In the first example, the passive voice removes the need to say who has actually refused the application.

There's something oddly dispiriting about the passive voice. It evokes the ghost of Franz Kafka and his world of weak individuals trapped in a landscape of callous, machinating, unfathomable bureaucracy. Maybe people in large organisations get to feel that their life is really like that – but they should not let this damage the way they communicate.

Should you go the whole way and never use a passive, ever? No, there are circumstances when it is useful.

- First, when someone has been the victim of circumstances and you wish to show the fact:

  Walking home from the pub, he was knocked down by a drunk driver.

Life does hand out random bits of bad luck to people, and the passive voice expresses this well.

- Second, the passive can help make paragraphs cohere. I'll talk more about this in the next chapter.

- Third, passives can get you out of the 'dangling participle' problem. Remember the sentence:

  Cycling along a path used by Dr Livingstone, a leopard leapt out and attacked me.

A passive will stop this sounding silly:

  Cycling along a path used by Dr Livingstone, I was attacked by a leopard.

- Fourth, you may genuinely not know the 'subject' of an action.

- And finally, yes, you may want to hide behind a passive voice. If this is the case, at least do so knowingly.

Use positive not negative verbs

When I teach writing, I say to the class:

- *Close your eyes . . .*

- *Don't think of a purple cow! Don't!*

Of course, everyone – or almost everyone – fails the 'task'. To get to the negative, one has to go via the positive, otherwise we don't know what to exclude from our thoughts. But why take this long route? Remember that our natural information-processing technique is to look for subject/verb/object and create some picture or model of it. If we then negate that, the subconscious will feel aggrieved. 'You made me build this model; now you're telling me to take it down again.'

I also feel that there's something more healthy about writing in the positive. Depressed people are often hemmed in with 'no's; psychologically healthy people in some deep sense say 'yes' to life. We brighten up in the company of a positive person; negative people are a turn-off. (There's a garage near where I live which has a set of 'don'ts' posted up on the door as you come in. They don't accept credit, or Scottish or £50 notes. No more than two children are allowed in at a time. Toilets are not to be used, except by customers. They won't give change for telephones or the air pump. I get my petrol somewhere else.)

Negatives get worse once they start stacking up. Double negatives can be hell to unscramble.

It is unusual for us not to do well in such circumstances.

Quickly, now – this means . . .

OK, you've all got there. But it takes time to work that out, and the reader's subconscious doesn't have time.

Double negatives can also be ambiguous. Grammatically, two negatives cancel each other out, as in the example above, but when someone on *EastEnders* says, '*I don't want nothing to do with it,*' the two negatives reinforce each other. Of course, you're educated people and won't make that mistake. But will your reader? Or *might* your reader? As always, don't leave small chinks for misunderstanding to seep through.

As with passives, I'm not saying 'never write in the negative'. For example, in safety instructions, where *Do not . . .* is required, use it:

> *Do not use this extinguisher in cases of electrical malfunction*

but provide users with a positive alternative as well:

> *– use the green one instead.*

What I am saying is 'use negatives sparingly, and only when you have to.'

Be as specific as you can

Fiction writers are always taught to be as specific as possible.

> *The woman got out of the car, put her bag over her shoulder and walked across the road*

tells you very little.

> *Estelle got out of the Porsche, slung her Prada bag over her shoulder and strutted across Millionaires' Row*

may not be great literature but it creates a picture. In non-fiction writing you are also in the business of creating pictures in your readers' minds. You may not have the freedom of the novelist (Gustave Flaubert was noted for agonising over the precise choice of individual words, but he had a private income and only wrote a handful of books in his life) but you should still look at every word you write and ask, 'Is this the most precise word I can find to describe what I'm saying?'

Of course, your ability to use specific words will increase as your vocabulary does, so . . .

Keep learning new words

This is *not* an injunction to go off and fill your writing with all sorts of exotic words that literary writers use, like *sussurate* (which means make a whispering sound like a gentle wind blowing through pine trees), *lambent* (radiant, but in an understated, rather British sort of way) or *flexure* (bending). It *is* an injunction to keep on building your working knowledge of the English language.

Read quality writing:

- Broadsheet not red-top newspapers.

- Well-written and well-edited magazines, such as *Prospect* or the *Economist*. (Even if you don't agree with their views, they express themselves well.)

- Well-written novels from any era, not cheap thrillers or romances. (This needn't be as wearisome as it sounds: many top British crime writers such as P.D. James and Ian Rankin write extremely well, and many prizewinning literary novels, UK,

Commonwealth and US alike, are actually less hard work than literary snobs make them out to be.)

- Quality non-fiction writing. There's some truly breathtaking stuff around, if you know where to find it. At the end of this book, I give a short list of my favourite texts: writing I turn to again and again to be delighted, exhilarated, inspired and generally reassured of the power and value of my chosen craft.

Find quality writers whom you particularly like, and read as much of their work as you can. You may find you begin to sound a bit like them as you write – that's fine. Rephrase any bits that strike you as too obviously borrowed, but otherwise, allow yourself to copy masters. Over time, you will develop your own voice and style.

Learning new words doesn't just mean looking them up in the dictionary. Do that, of course, but be aware that the definition(s) you find will only be your introduction to the word, a bit like when a hostess at a party takes you across to someone and says in a couple of sentences what they do. You have a lot of exploring and learning to do before the word becomes something you truly know how to use, just as it will take time to get to know the new person.

Here are three questions to ask when getting to know a new word:

1. What are its implications, its echoes? Does it carry a whiff of disapproval or imply authorial approbation? (When we go *travelling*, we find other *tourists* a bit of a pain, and hope we won't have the misfortune to come across any *trippers*...) Does it have historical references that might be unfortunate? For example, the term 'cultural revolution' gets bandied about, but

actually refers to one of the most barbaric events of the last century.

2. Is it only used in certain contexts? If so, what are they? Literary? Technical?

3. How well known is it? If it turns out to be obscure, keep it for early drafts, or for attempts at more literary work, or for one of those moments beloved of all true writers, when you know this is the only word that sums up exactly what you want to say, so it has to go in.

Keep asking these questions as you come across the new word in different contexts. At the same time, experiment with it in the early drafting of your own work. The first few times, it may feel clunky or somehow wrong – go with that awareness and replace it. Then suddenly you'll find you are using it with confidence.

It's a bit like learning to use a complicated new piece of machinery or a sophisticated software program. Take your time.

Use simile, metaphor and analogy

A **simile** is a poetic, imaginative comparison between one thing and another, the classic example being Burns'

> *My love is like a red, red rose.*

A **metaphor** is a more condensed version of this, where the comparison has been turned into a word in the main phrase:

> *The castle was perched on an outcrop overlooking the town* (birds perch; castles only do so 'metaphorically').

An **analogy** is when one understood concept or process is used to explain another, mysterious concept or process by pointing out similarities. A clear (though apparently now outdated) example is the old model of the atom I learned at school, where the analogy was drawn between an atom and the solar system, both having a huge, energised body at the core and much, much smaller entities whizzing round it in circular orbits. A good analogy is an unbeatable short-cut to making sense of the baffling – though of course all analogies eventually 'break down', sounding silly if you push them too far. (Electrons don't have tiny little people living on them.)

Here's George Orwell:

> *A man may take to drink because he feels himself to be a failure, and then fail all the more completely because he drinks. It is rather the same thing with the English language. It becomes ugly and inaccurate because our thoughts are foolish, but the slovenliness of our language makes it easier for us to have foolish thoughts.*

A thought-provoking analogy, expressed in clear, precise language (and thoughts with which I totally agree – do read his essay 'Politics and the English Language').

Similes and metaphors are more tools for the artistic writer – the novelist, the poet, the dramatist – than the non-fiction writer, but if you can work them into your non-fiction without sounding pretentious then you should do so. It makes the writing fresh and interesting. When I co-authored a book on how to start and build a business, we needed to find a word to describe the key team members you needed to get on board. I guess I could have called them that – key team members, or even KTMs, which would have gone down well in business schools – but neither I nor my co-author, a down-to-earth salesman/entrepreneur, liked that way of speaking, so we used a metaphor. These people (experts in sales, finance and the relevant technology) were the *cornerstones* of the business. The result was a clear, strong, evocative image – cornerstones are strong, solid, 'four-square' and create the foundations of the business. Take them away and the business collapses.

Similarly Geoffrey Moore, who has a degree in English as well as being a business guru, wrote a book about the problems facing technology companies as they move from selling to tech-heads to selling to ordinary customers. Rather than blather on about 'mass market entry strategies' he called this move *crossing the chasm*, and his book has sold in vast numbers.

In fact, much of the language we use every day started as original, imaginative metaphors (a remarkable number of them Shakespeare's) and then bedded down as standard usage.

Uncritical use of standard metaphors can lead to 'mixed metaphors', and unintentionally comic lines such as:

> *The government has tried to grab the bull by the horns but has ended up with egg on its face.*

It sounds like they made a pig's ear of the whole thing . . .

Sports commentators seem to be drawn to mixed metaphors like particularly gullible moths to extra-bright candles. Among my favourites are:

> *I think the big guns will come to the boil today.*

> *That's another nail in his afternoon . . .*

> *They've tasted the other side of the coin on many occasions.*

> *We haven't had the rub of the dice.*

> *It was that game that put the Everton ship back on the road.*

Read through those again, and really savour the surreal imagery!

It isn't just sports people who fall into this trap. Former prime ministers can do it, too. Here's John Major:

> *When your back's against the wall it's time to turn round and fight.*

And, of course, no collection of metaphor mixing by politicians would be complete without the master surrealist, George W. Bush:

> *Free societies will be allies against the hateful few who kill at the whim of a hat.*

Another amusing mishandling of metaphors is the misuse of the word *literally* in conjunction with them. *Literally*, of course, means, 'No, I'm not using a metaphor here, I really mean it' – but I endlessly come across comments like:

> *The audience were literally glued to their seats*

or

> *The boys came home literally legless.*

As with all true surrealism, we are swept from joyful absurdity to bizarre cruelty in a moment. Long may this type of writing continue – but not by you, please.

Be assertive

T.S. Eliot once wrote a piece called 'Notes towards a definition of culture'. He didn't mean this; he meant, 'Here's what I think culture is all about.' Why did he engage in this false modesty? When he wrote poetry, he was much more upfront. Would anyone have read *The Land, which some people might describe as being a tiny bit 'Waste'* or *Some Quartets, I think there are somewhere between three and five of them*?

If you've got something to say, say it! Cut out those phrases like *should like to, we will try to, we wish to inform you*:

> *We wish to inform you that your January payment is overdue.*

No.

> *Your January payment is overdue.*

Some people think the former is more polite, but I don't really see that. Communication should always be polite, but shouldn't pussy-foot about. The point is not to turn every piece of writing into a table-thumping manifesto, but to remember that people are taking time out of their busy lives to read what you write. If all you're saying is, 'Actually, I'm not sure about *x*. It could be *a* or it could be *b*, and some people even think it's *c* . . .' are you wasting that time?

Use Anglo-Saxon not Latinate words

This is a common piece of advice in 'how-to-write' books, and I largely endorse it. The basis of our language is Anglo-Saxon: the words for what we see about us (features of landscape, plants and animals), parts of the body, colours, verbs of feeling and action, 'auxiliary verbs' (must, ought etc.), and most pronouns, prepositions, conjunctions and determiners. The hundred most used words in English are all Anglo-Saxon, as are all those crazy-to-pronounce words like through, thought, thorough, bough, cough, dough, hiccough etc. Oh, and most of our rude words as well . . .

However, English isn't just updated Anglo-Saxon but a wonderful mixture of influences. Did you know that *orange* comes from Sanskrit? Or that *capsize* comes from Catalan? Or that *magic* comes from Avestan, a now extinct language spoken in ancient Persia? (Do visit a website called KryssTal for more fascinating facts about etymology, the study of word origins.)

I have already recommended perpetually working on stretching your vocabulary. Clearly you can't do this if you stick only to Anglo-Saxon. The real force of the 'Anglo-Saxon, not Latinate' rule is not to propose a kind of linguistic chauvinism, but to warn against an opposite, but equally silly, mistake – that of long-word snobbery. *Initiate* is not somehow classier than *begin*, any more than a knitted-doll loo-roll cover is classier than an unadorned roll quietly placed where it is most useful.

Prune

I have some roses in my garden, and during the summer they sprout loads of shoots. Over the winter, these have to be pruned. One year I forgot, or was too lazy, and the rose was a complete mess the next year, full of small, twiggy bits but with few flowers. Writing needs the same treatment.

Pruning is a great 'second-draft' activity. Get stuff down in the first draft; get pruning in the second. What should you look to cut out?

Obviously, those three big monsters, **ambiguity**, **repetition** and **jargon**. And, following the advice above, look to cut out **indecisiveness**.

Beginners often overuse **adjectives**, thinking they add colour to a piece. Adjectives certainly do this, but only if well chosen and sharp, as they are in this example from Thomas Hobbes, writing during the English Civil War about life in a state of anarchy:

> *There is no place for Industry, because the fruit thereof is uncertain, and consequently no culture of the earth; no Navigation, nor the use of the commodities that may be imported by Sea; no commodious Building, no Instruments of moving and removing things that require much force, no Knowledge of the face of the Earth, no account of Time, no Arts, no Letters, no Society and, which is worst of all, continual fear and danger of violent death, and the life of man is solitary, poor, nasty, brutish and short.*

This is surely one of the greatest sentences in the English language, building slowly up through a list that grows ever snappier and more vicious, and culminating in those five adjectives that hit you like five punches from a heavyweight boxer.

Most adjective use is more like a tickle from a rather mangy feather, however.

The job of adjectives is to qualify nouns, in other words to say something specific about a noun, to make it different from other nouns of its type. To give an obvious example, blue cars are a subset of all cars, distinguished from red ones or green ones by – well, I'm sure you get the point . . .

Dull adjectives don't do this job. They are often either tautological or clichéd.

- A tautology says the same thing twice, as in *wet water*, *new innovation* etc.

- Clichés are weary old phrases that everyone knows and which tell us nothing new. I'm not totally against them; the odd old favourite can keep readers content. But unending strings of them signal that the writer has given no thought to what they're saying (or that they have, but are a particularly bad writer). Clichéd adjectives we've all heard are things like: *bated breath*, *extensive views* (estate agents are masters of cliché – no doubt the extensive views were *boasted* by the property), *tender mercies*, *psychological moment* etc.

Remember the Golden Rule: examine all your words and ask yourself if they really do lead your reader forward.

Harness the power of threes

Powerful writing often uses words in threes. Here is Katherine Chidley, petitioning Oliver Cromwell:

> *We think ourselves bound to hinder that, after the abundant calamities which have overspread all quarters of the land, the change be only notional, nominal, circumstantial, while the real burdens, grievances and bondages be continued.*

And here's Edmund Burke:

The age of chivalry has gone: the age of economists,
sophists and calculators has arrived.

I don't know why these threes are so powerful, but they are. Maybe it's because we see in three dimensions, and feel that a 'two-dimensional' picture of something is somehow incomplete and unfulfilling, or because to get an accurate assessment of something's position we have to triangulate – two readings aren't enough.

Of course the threes mustn't be tautologous. If, in trying to harness the power of threes, we describe someone as nasty, unpleasant and not nice, we're simply repeating ourselves. Really good threes all throw light on the subject from different angles, creating – I have to come back to it – a truly three-dimensional picture.

Here's Edward Gibbon, triangulating perfectly:

The historian is . . . surrounded with imperfect
fragments, always concise, often obscure, and
sometimes contradictory.

Like any writing tool, the power of threes is not to be overused. If every noun comes qualified with three adjectives, the pattern soon becomes predictable and boring. And if there are really only one or two things you want to say about something, then say them and move on, rather than searching around for a third. When Churchill talked about **famous ancient** *states now prostrate under the Nazi yoke*, those two adjectives were quite sufficient to sum up a whole picture of distinctive and important traditions being trampled under a jackboot.

The power of threes is not only about choice of words. Storytellers use the power of threes at the next level, to set up expectations then surprise us. One occurrence of an event is an instance; two is a pattern; which sets up the opportunity to confound the expectation at the third occurrence.

Be funny – if you know it will work

This goes against the advice given in all communication courses, which resolutely tell you to cut out the humour. But people like humour, and if you can make them laugh gently, then you'll be even more of a pleasure to read.

Clearly there have to be some riders:

- You must know your audience . . .

- . . . and know that they find you funny. Sadly, some people think they are funny but just aren't. If you're not getting the laughs, then cut the comedy.

- Remember that the wider a message gets spread, the wider range of tastes it will encounter. Something that makes you and your mates roar with laughter may upset someone else, which is fine as long as the communication only goes as far as your mates. But if it goes further, or *might* go further . . .

- The most effective humour to use is that directed at oneself, or, at the other extreme, at the general ironies of life. Laughs at the expense of any social group, race or nationality will probably cause offence, and are best avoided – though as an intelligent person reading this book, you're probably not into that sort of humour anyway.

Be original whenever you can

This instruction may cause frissons of fear in corporate readers. It shouldn't: I'm not advocating ripping up company handbooks and style manuals. Where there are house rules, stick to them (though the best in-house writers always manage to be more creative within those rules than the plodders). But for those of you not constrained by such rules, or who are only constrained by them some of the time – be original!

The greatest aid to originality is not LSD or opium, but the drafting process. It helps you to be original in two stages.

In your first draft, you can experiment. If you don't like what you've written, cross it out and try again. If you're not sure, leave it for the moment. When you do your second draft, if you feel that the experiment hasn't worked, you can remove it.

But actually the main benefit of the drafting process is that you can be more creative second time round. Often a first draft is about getting information down as quickly as you can. On rereading, you may find either that you have copied something direct from another source or that you unintentionally sound like someone else's writing. No problem: you now have the chance to re-express it your way. If you want to keep the borrowed material, that's fine – put it in quotes and acknowledge it, seeking permission if necessary. But otherwise, rework it and make the material your own.

How one develops a writing style is a mysterious process. It happens over time: the more you write, and read, the more you develop your own 'voice'. But you have to allow yourself to experiment in order for this process to occur.

This leads naturally to the most important advice of all:

Practise

Anyone who is good at anything practises. Top sportspeople, musicians . . . and writers. But also good amateur sportspeople, musicians and writers.

Truman Capote once said the only way to learn to write was to lock yourself in a room with a typewriter and write for ten years. (Capote also came up with the best put-down of rubbish writing I know. How often have I seen a piece of managementese and wanted to quote his wonderful line: 'That's not writing, that's typing.')

You may well ask, 'Write what for ten years?' The answer is, 'Anything.' Just like jogging: you don't have to run along a particular route to get fit; you do have to get out and run. So keep a journal, write a 'blog', write letters to friends – do anything to get the writing 'muscles' limbered up. What you will actually be doing is training your brain to go and fetch words out of the word-bank in your mind, and also to look at the words you have dug out, review them, and look for better words if necessary.

Of course, if you can practise your writing at work, all the better. You're getting paid for it then.

As with any programme of skill development, don't expect instant results, and do enjoy the journey. The truth is that the journey never ends. I've been in this game for twenty years, and I'm still learning and enjoying learning.

Lively writing

- Use the active voice, not the passive.

- Use positive verbs, not negative ones.

- Be as specific as you can.

- Keep learning new words.

- Use simile, metaphor and analogy.

- Be assertive.

- Use Anglo-Saxon, not Latinate words.

- Prune.

- Harness the power of threes.

- Be funny – if you know it will work.

- Be original whenever you can.

- Practise!

7 Style – sentences and paragraphs

The two previous chapters were essentially, though not totally, about choosing and using the right word(s) in the right way. But there is more to style than this; style is also about crafting sentences and paragraphs.

Complex sentences

As kids, we probably all wrote essays that followed the pattern below:

> *What we did on our holidays by Chris*
>
> *We packed our cases. We got in the car. We drove to Brighton. Jenny was sick twice. We parked outside the hotel. We went in. A man in a peaked cap stuck a piece of paper on our window. Daddy had an argument with him. The man telephoned the police. Two policemen came to see us . . .*

And so on. Strings of simple sentences. As we got older, our style improved and we made the sentences more complex, by:

• using conjunctions

We packed our cases and got in the car.

- using colons or semicolons

   We drove to Brighton; Jenny was sick twice.

- creating subordinate clauses

   When a man in a peaked cap stuck a piece of paper on our window, Daddy had an argument with him.

You might also include a fragment to make a particular section vivid:

   Jenny was sick. Twice.

Let's say a grown-up version becomes:

   We packed our cases, got in the car and drove to Brighton. Jenny was sick – twice. We parked outside the hotel and went in. A man in a peaked cap stuck a piece of paper on our window. Daddy had an argument with him. The man telephoned the police, and two officers came to see us . . .

In writing the above I did the following:

- Bundled dull but necessary information into single sentences – for example, sentence one gets us to Brighton.

- Kept more interesting sentences solitary, to heighten their effect.

- Expanded one simple sentence with the semi-comic dash.

I hope the piece now has more momentum and energy. It's still not going to win the Booker Prize, but it's an improvement.

One obvious improvement is that in the original piece, the sentences are all roughly the same length, whereas now there's more variety. This in itself is good. Badly written work tends to use the same length of sentence over and over again, and the effect is incredibly boring.

Here's a piece of travel writing that varies sentence lengths nicely:

> *A grey plain stretched out in front of me, windswept and unpopulated, apart from a small queue at Chairman Mao's mausoleum and a few knots of tourists and vendors. Round the edges ran four-lane boulevards. These were just as empty, except for one Red Flag limousine and a clutch of jangling cyclists making their way past the long, low roofs of Tiananmen (the Gate of Heavenly Peace, from which the Square takes its name) at the far end. By the concrete pillar of the Revolutionary Martyrs' Memorial stood a line of flagpoles. They were unadorned, their halyards slapping idly in the wind, making a cold, lonely noise that filled this place and made it sound like a British seaside resort in winter.*

That's 29, 7, 43, 13 and 30 words.

A danger with complex sentences is that they become *too* complex, and the reader gets lost. Apparently the average sentence length in professionally written non-fiction material is 17 words. This shouldn't be taken as a 'rule' – the average length of a sentence in the piece above is 24, and it reads fine – but if you are constantly way over that figure, then your sentences are probably too long for your readers.

Two particular problems in over-long sentences are nests of subordinate clauses and strings of 'ands'.

Subordinate clause overload

> *A pterodactyl, which is a winged reptile from the Triassic era, which lasted from 248 to 206 million years ago and saw the rise of the dinosaurs, is not to be confused, as often happens, with the archaeopteryx, which evolved in a later era, the Jurassic, and is the true evolutionary ancestor of modern birds, being covered with feathers.*

Interesting stuff, but hard work.

A basic rule in sentence construction is to get the subject and the main verb on to the page quickly, so the reader knows what the sentence is about and what sort of action we are talking about. If you can get to the object quickly, too, that's an added bonus: we have our basic picture in place, and can now elaborate on it in a certain amount of comfort.

The basic point of the above morass is 'the pterodactyl is not to be confused with the archaeopteryx'. So why not say that first? Then we have to order the rest of the information, of course. Our old friends 'the former' and 'the latter' look good candidates here. And don't be afraid to break up a long sentence . . .

> *The pterodactyl is not to be confused with the archaeopteryx, a mistake often made. The former is a winged reptile from the Triassic era, which lasted from 248 to 206 million years ago and saw the rise of the dinosaurs; the latter evolved in a later era, the Jurassic, and is the true evolutionary ancestor of modern birds, being covered with feathers.*

You might want to sort out the clunky sound in the middle – *the latter evolved in a later era.* Use a synonym: *the latter evolved in a subsequent era . . .*

This rule ('get subject, verb, object down as quickly as possible') is a great way of sorting out sentences that have been flooded by subordinate clauses, but it is not a rule to observe all the time. In the piece of travel writing, the author varies the shape of the sentences so as not to sound repetitive. However, note that it's the shorter sentences that have been turned round (*Round the edges ran four-lane boulevards . . .*). The longer the sentence, the riskier it is to depart from the rule.

Strings of 'and's

The innocuous conjunction *and* can land poor writers in all kinds of mess. Here's a piece of Dalek writing:

> *Implementation of Strategy B will ensure consistency of application and ongoing improvements of processes and systems across process and business boundaries.*

There's a lot to say about this, almost all of it uncomplimentary. For now, let's just look at the *and*s. What does the writer mean?

It could be that the strategy will ensure three things:

- *consistency of application*
- *ongoing improvements of processes*
- *ongoing improvements of systems*

all of these *across process and business boundaries.*

Or two things:

- *consistency of application of processes and systems*
- *ongoing improvements of processes and systems*

both of these *across two kinds of boundary, process and business.*
    Or even:

- *consistency of application*

and two other things:

- *ongoing improvements of processes*
- *ongoing improvements of systems*

both of these *across two kinds of boundary, process and business.*
    Or some other combination? I think the answer is the middle one – but we've had to sit and scratch our heads to work it out. And that's bad writing.
    Assuming the middle one is correct, how could it be phrased better? One way is to use bullet points:

> *Implementation of Strategy B will ensure:*
>
> - *consistency of application*
> - *ongoing improvements*
>
> *of processes and systems, across process and business boundaries.*

Alternatively, use the word *both*, plus a well-placed comma:

> *Implementation of Strategy B will ensure both*
> *consistency of application and ongoing improvements of*
> *processes and systems, across process and business*
> *boundaries.*

Of course, the language remains obscure and flabby. But at least the sentence now has a proper, unambiguous shape.

Let's leave the world of management for something nicer.

> *Joanne had the most beautiful eyes I had ever seen,*
> *flame-red hair and a smile that was joyful and life-*
> *enhancing and I fell in love with her in five minutes.*

Delightful, but overloaded with *and*s. How do we get round this? It's a bit unromantic to use bullet points:

> *Joanne had:*
>
> • *the most beautiful eyes I had ever seen*
>
> • *flame-red hair*
>
> • *a smile that was joyful and life-enhancing*
>
> *and I fell in love with her in five minutes.*

Though at least if we did that the sentence would be clear. So what can we do?

Back to basics: first, find the pivot of the sentence – obviously, here, it's before *and I.* So let's put a break in here. A semicolon? I'd go further, and split the sentence into two.

> *Joanne had the most beautiful eyes I had ever seen,*
> *flame-red hair and a smile that was joyful and life-*
> *enhancing. I fell in love with her in five minutes.*

This leaves us with two *and*s near the end of the first sentence, which is not disastrous but does leave room for temporary confusion: when readers see the second *and*, they are tempted to wonder if a fourth attribute of Joanne is coming up (*and a very rich daddy*) or another attribute of her smile. So let's remove this potential confusion by using *both*:

> *Joanne had the most beautiful eyes I had ever seen,*
> *flame-red hair and a smile that was both joyful and*
> *life-enhancing. I fell in love with her in five minutes.*

Five minutes? It took that long?

The beauty of balance

Arguably the most beautifully balanced prose was written in the eighteenth century. However, this does not mean that balance is 'out of date'. Far from it – though when looking for examples, I was driven back to the master of balance, Edward Gibbon, and his wonderful *The Decline and Fall of the Roman Empire*. Here are the opening lines:

> *In the second century of the Christian era, the empire of*
> *Rome comprehended the fairest part of the earth and*
> *the most civilized portion of mankind. The frontiers of*
> *that extensive monarchy were guarded by ancient*
> *renown and disciplined valour.*

Perfect balance!

> *the fairest part of the earth* ↔ *the most civilized portion*
> *of mankind*
>
> *ancient renown* ↔ *disciplined valour*

Both those contrasts pivot on the word *and*. Other conjunctions – *but* is the classic one – can be used to make what I call a 'contrasting balance'. (*She was poor but she was honest.*) Gibbon uses a string of these to demolish an obscure later Roman emperor, Carinus.

> *In the Gallic war, he discovered some degree of*
> *personal courage; but from the moment of his arrival*
> *in Rome he abandoned himself to the luxury of the*
> *capital and the abuse of his fortune. He was soft yet*
> *cruel, devoted to pleasure but destitute of taste, and*
> *though exquisitely susceptible of vanity, indifferent to*
> *the public esteem.*

A contrasting balance doesn't have to have conjunctions: it can pivot around a colon or semicolon. I was delighted when a former writing student sent me a programme she'd written for an exhibition of some of her artwork. Her last sentence ran:

> *The paintings on show here are in bright, clear colours,*
> *the colour of happy dreams: my nightmares I keep in*
> *the portfolio.*

I felt a real tingle of pleasure reading that perfect piece of contrasting balance.

The opposite of balanced writing is, rather obviously, imbalanced writing. I have covered grammatically incorrect imbalance (*We require students of either French or native speakers*), but there can also be imbalanced but grammatically correct writing. Though it won't upset any grammarians, this is still bad writing. Imagine a rewrite of Gibbon's opening:

> *In the second century of the Christian era, the empire of Rome comprehended the fairest part of the earth and lots of people.*

Worse than being clunky, imbalanced writing can be unclear:

> *At the animal shelter we found black cats and dogs.*

Black cats and black dogs, or black cats and dogs of all sorts of colours? Answer, probably, the former. But probably isn't good enough. Readers don't want 'probably'; they want clarity.

> *At the animal shelter we found dogs and black cats*

will do it. Better still, because more equally balanced, is:

> *At the animal shelter we found dogs of all colourings and black cats.*

I say 'equally balanced' because

> *Dogs of all colourings ↔ black cats*

has a noun and an adjective (or adjective phrase) on each 'arm' of the balance. Note that in this example, the balancing pairs have been 'switched round'.

> Noun (*dogs*) + adjective   ↔   adjective (*black*) + noun
> phrase (*of all colours*)   (*cats*).

This is a neat and very old trick, technically called 'chiasmus'.

If you want to stress that you were looking for a marmalade cat and were disappointed, then use a contrasting balance and write:

> *At the animal shelter we found dogs of all colourings*
> *but only black cats.*

Ending sentences effectively

The standard wisdom is that the beginning of a sentence sets the scene, and the end is where you 'pay off' the sentence by making your most emphatic comment.

> *Climate change will cause flooding and other forms of*
> *land degradation, bringing about massive economic*
> *disruption, involuntary migration and probably the*
> *deaths of millions of people.*

As with most rules, this must not become a slavish orthodoxy, otherwise your writing will become predictable and dull. The end of a sentence is often a good place for a jokey aside, and can also be a good place to set up a link to the next sentence. (More on linking in the paragraphs on 'flow' below.)

The 'end with emphasis' rule is probably used more invariably in rhetoric, as in Churchill's 'fight on the beaches' speech or Hobbes' description of life in an anarchic society.

Paragraphs

As with sentences, the topic of a paragraph should usually be announced at the beginning. It doesn't have to be the first word – though often is, for example in a heading. But after the first sentence of a paragraph, the reader should be thinking, 'This paragraph is about x.'

As with sentences, good writers will play with this rule: some paragraphs will have a build-up in the early sentences leading to the key point around the middle. Other paragraphs will keep the reader puzzled till the end – what I call a 'Milk Tray' paragraph, after those ads where you see a chap diving off a rock, fighting a shark, scaling a cliff, breaking into a house guarded by Rottweilers *and all because the lady loves Milk Tray*. But these are interesting exceptions rather than the rule.

Just as with sentences, the end of the paragraph is a place of maximum emphasis.

Unity

Poor paragraphs wander off the point. They do this because halfway through the paragraph the writer is reminded of something interesting to say, and hares off in pursuit of this exciting new line of thought. This is, after all, what we often do in conversation. And, actually, in a first draft, it's not a bad thing to do, as it can open up new perspectives. The failure lies in not editing the paragraph later: the interesting digression needs to be taken back under the writer's control.

For example:

> *The roads in the Highlands are gradually being improved,*
> *but sections still deteriorate into single-track lanes with*
> *'passing places'. This can even be true of A-class roads,*
> *such as the A838 north of Laxford Bridge or around Loch*

Eriboll. Loch Eriboll is a deep sea-loch, which was used during the last war as an anchorage by the Royal Navy. Despite its magnificent surroundings, the loch was referred to as Loch 'Orrible by the sailors, presumably because of the dearth of things to do there. In May 1945, the German U-boat fleet surrendered in its waters.

The surrender of the German U-boat fleet is probably more interesting than the state of the A838, but the fact is that the paragraph begins with a discussion of the condition of Highland roads, and should stick to that topic. You're breaking a promise to the reader, otherwise.

One solution would be to break the one paragraph into two, after the first mention of Loch Eriboll, but the reader would still be buffeted around – first we have a paragraph about roads, then one about a loch. It would be better to move the Eriboll paragraph elsewhere, once you've said all you need to say about roads and have clearly signalled to the reader that it's time to move on to a new topic. This also would give you more freedom to tell us about Loch Eriboll. I'd like to know more about the surrender. How many U-boats actually sailed into the loch to surrender? Who signed the document? Are there any eyewitness accounts?

An alternative would be to put the Loch Eriboll section in brackets. Some people disapprove of this, but it seems fine to me, provided it's not overdone. The brackets tell the reader there's a digression coming up; you digress; then you get back to the main topic. The limitation of this is that you can't say very much – a brief digression is fine, a long one is tedious; you must, of course, return to your main topic in the next paragraph.

Using passives for unity

Consider this passage:

> *The next stop on our journey is Harlech. Owain Glyndwr, the Welsh landlord who rebelled against Henry IV, captured Harlech Castle and held Welsh parliaments here from 1404 to 1409. During the Wars of the Roses in the same century, Yorkist troops besieged the castle. Experts say that the song 'Men of Harlech' dates from this time. During the Civil War, Royalist troops were besieged in the castle, and its fall marked the end of Charles I's resistance to Cromwell's forces.*

There's nothing hugely wrong with it, but it feels a bit flabby and 'unworked'. A major reason for this is that there is a variety of subjects in the various sentences in the paragraph (the next stop, Owain Glyndwr, Yorkist troops, experts, Royalist troops), which (apart from two lots of troops) don't have a lot in common, other than the fact that none of them is the actual topic that the paragraph is supposed to be about! Tighten the paragraph up by changing the sentence subjects, bringing them closer in meaning both to each other and to the topic of the paragraph. How? You will recall that I said in Chapter 6 that a use for the passive voice would be to help paragraphs cohere. Well, here it is in action:

> *The next stop on our journey is Harlech. Harlech Castle was captured by Owain Glyndwr, the Welsh landlord who rebelled against Henry IV and who used Harlech for Welsh parliaments from 1404 to 1409. During the Wars of the Roses in the same*

> *century, it was besieged by Yorkist troops: the song*
> *'Men of Harlech' is said to date from this time.*
> *During the Civil War, it was besieged by the*
> *Parliamentarians, and its fall marked the end of*
> *Charles I's resistance.*

That feels better – more united, more under control. The sentence subjects are now the next stop, Harlech Castle, it (clearly the castle), it (also clearly the castle). As a result, we feel confident the paragraph is about Harlech and its (splendid – do visit it) castle and will stay about Harlech and its castle, and that we won't get led away into a discussion about Owain Glyndwr or the Wars of the Roses. There is now also scope for some extra comment about the castle to be worked into the text, something that would have rendered the 'active verb' version horrifically clumsy, but which slots into the passive verb version with ease. I mean something like:

> *The next stop on our journey is Harlech. Harlech*
> *Castle, magnificently situated on a rock overlooking the*
> *town and the sea, was captured . . .*

Flow

As well as having unity, paragraphs should flow, taking the reader gently along.

The paragraph about the A838 that suddenly turned into a piece on Loch Eriboll did at least flow nicely from the proper topic into the digression:

> *This can even be true of A-class roads, such as the A838*
> *north of Laxford Bridge or around Loch Eriboll. Loch*
> *Eriboll is a deep sea-loch . . .*

Bad writing often doesn't even do the reader the politeness of digressing elegantly – it just leaps from one idea to another, leaving the reader lost and wondering what on earth has happened. An example of this would be if the above section had read:

> *This can even be true of A-class roads, such as the A838*
> *north of Laxford Bridge. Loch Eriboll is a deep sea-loch . . .*

If we look into the writer's train of thought, we would probably see a hidden logic:

> *Worst bits of the A838. The bit north of Laxford Bridge.*
> *Then there's the bit round Loch Eriboll. Loch Eriboll is*
> *an interesting place, by the way. Did you know . . .*

Yes, there is a route in the *writer's* mind from one topic to the next, but the writer has not shown it to the reader.

When I started writing PR copy, still full of plans to be a novelist and rather keen on the 'stream of consciousness' style of James Joyce and Virginia Woolf, I tended to hide links, thinking it was clever and artistic to do so. My boss often looked at my copy and said, 'There's a thought missing there.' He was almost always right.

There's an excellent discussion of unity and flow in paragraphs in *Style: The Basics of Clarity and Grace* by Joseph M. Williams, a short but wise book I highly recommend.

Flow between paragraphs

Though a paragraph introduces a new topic or viewpoint, it's still nice to be led gently into it (usually, anyway – as with all style rules, slavish obedience to them makes writing dull). Hence the use of what grammarians call 'metadiscourse', odd words or phrases like *however, moreover, on the other hand* that often begin paragraphs, relating them back to what the reader has read and teeing them up for what's going to come.

Informal numbering is metadiscourse. The writer says, *There are four reasons why the UK should embrace the euro*, then goes on to give the four reasons, each one having its own paragraph. Try and vary your metadiscourse here – don't just say *Firstly . . . Secondly . . . Thirdly . . . Fourthly . . .* at the start of each respective paragraph. If you just once say something like *A third reason is . . .* you've livened things up enormously. Most important of all, please make sure you pay off the promise. The number of times I've read pieces that talk about, say, 'five factors', and begin by enumerating them (*The first is . . . Secondly . . .*) then leave readers to search around for the other three. It's infuriating!

Some metadiscourse can be rejected as waffle, like the public speaker who *thinks he can say, without fear of contradiction . . .* , but much metadiscourse is actually very useful in leading the reader over the gap that can open up between paragraphs.

Of course, sometimes you do leap to a new subject. You've said all you need to say about x, now it's time for y. So tell the reader about the leap. You could put in some metadiscourse along the lines of, *Now, on to a new topic . . .* I often do this at the start of chapters – possibly unnecessarily, but I like to feel it's a politeness to the reader.

Or simply use headings. These tell the reader clearly and simply that the old topic is done and a new one about to begin. They also tell the reader what that new topic is going to be. What could be more helpful than that? Some writers seem to fight shy of headings.

Don't. They help you to organise your thoughts, and your readers to organise theirs. They inspire confidence in your readers that you have marshalled the relevant information and that you are in control of their journey from being uninformed to being informed

Paragraphs

- Focus

  - Make the paragraph about something

  - Tell the reader early on what the paragraph is about

  - Don't wander off the subject

- Keep the sentences united!

  - Keep the subjects of most sentences related to the paragraph topic

  - Use passives if necessary

- Flow, don't jump – make the necessary links between thoughts

- Use 'metadiscourse' to fill in the gaps between paragraphs

- Vary paragraph lengths

  - Three to six sentences is average

Paragraph length

As with sentences, keep paragraph lengths varied. Most paragraphs in professionally written work are between three and six sentences long, but that's a big generalisation. What is undoubted is that paragraphs have been getting shorter over the years. Open Orwell's essays from the 1930s and 40s, and sometimes a page will be just one big paragraph. I can't think of any good modern non-fiction writer who would do that. Instead, things have probably gone too far the other way.

Especially in advertising.

But you're not planning to write like that.

Are you?

No? Good. The odd one-sentence para is fine, of course, but it will draw attention to itself, so should be used rarely, for making an emphatic point.

Sections

For many pieces of non-fiction, sections are the next level up from paragraphs. In essence the rules are similar to those for paragraphs:

- make them about something

- tell the reader clearly and quickly what they are about

- don't wander off the subject

- keep a natural flow going.

One difference: the good writer consciously varies the length of paragraphs and sentences, but not of sections. Actually, the opposite is true: well-balanced pieces of work have sections of similar lengths, which show that their authors have broken down the material into chunks of roughly similar sizes.

How sections fit together is essentially a matter of *structure*, which I will deal with in the next chapter, when talking about planning. The time has come to get writing!

8 Getting it done – audience, planning and structure

Well, it's *almost* time to get writing. First of all, you need to think about your audience and to do some planning. Or, to put it more snappily:

- Think 'reader'
- Plan.

Think 'reader'

I've used the word 'communication' throughout this book. Remember the implications of this: there are people at the receiving end of what you are communicating, and if they don't understand what you are trying to say, your attempt at communication has failed, however brilliant you thought it was.

So, the first question you must ask yourself is, 'Who is going to read this?'

'Lots of different people' is not a good enough answer. If the answer is a lot of people, then ask yourself what they have in common. Think like a marketer. If their audience is a diverse one, marketers subdivide them into meaningful sub-groups and then aim subtly different communications at each sub-group.

This is called 'segmenting'. You should do the same for your readers . . .

. . . if you have to. Luckily, much communication is aimed at a single audience. For example, a manual for a new piece of software for a bank will only be read by employees of that bank, and only by employees at a certain level. A sales report might be aimed at members of a board. A piece in the parish magazine is for village residents. Yes, you may say, but 'village residents' means everyone from the retired colonel in the Old Manse to the farmhand in a tied house – not to mention the old lady in Lilac Cottage who keeps solving murders that have the CID baffled. But consider what they all have in common. They will share both a concern for the village's welfare and a set of references: you don't need to explain that St Barnabas' is the local church.

Having segmented their audience, marketers often go on to imagine an ideal model listener, an 'archetype'. You should do the same. Having established that the software manuals are going to be read by a bank manager, the report by the chairman, the maga-zine piece by someone who lives in one of those new houses on The Close, then go further: give these archetypes names and faces. Sometimes that's easy: the chairman is the chairman. But imagine the manual-reading bank manager. She's aged 45, married with three children, is educated to degree level. More important, she is busy; she doesn't know about software; she doesn't want to know about software; and she is rather aggrieved at having to master this new thing on her computer when the old one was perfectly all right.

Imagine the archetype actually reading what you have written. Ask some questions.

Have you got credibility with this person?

Yes? Good. Don't waste it. Having credibility will make this reader give you a little more time, but if you start boring or baffling them, then that advantage will soon be squandered.

No? You need to establish it, fast. Readers need to know why they should expend their scarce, valuable resources of time and attention on you – and they need to know it quickly, or they'll tune out.

If you're writing a letter, explain why you are writing to that person. The explanation needs to be centred round your perception of the reader's needs and interests, not your needs and interests. Cynically, every reader asks, 'What's in it for me?'

If the reader is an acquaintance, remind them of your point of contact.

What does the reader know already?

This is crucial. We've already seen in the discussion on jargon that what to the insider is clear, appropriate use of technical terms is gobbledegook to the outsider. Sadly, most recipients are somewhere in between: much non-fiction writing is a balancing act, on a pretty narrow ridge between two steep drops, over-explaining on one side and baffling with technical terms on the other. There's no set formula for getting it right. Keep thinking about your typical reader, and what your best guess is as to what that person knows.

In borderline cases, you can say things like, *Most of you probably know this already, but for any reader who doesn't . . .*

My experience is that the more knowledgeable you become about a subject, the more likely you are to overestimate other people's knowledge of it. So err on the side of explaining and simplicity.

What does the reader need to know?

In any workplace document, this question is crucial. Outside the workplace, you can relax a little, and simply ask, 'What would the reader like to know?'

Sadly, huge numbers of 'communicators' fail to ask either of these questions, and instead ask a rather different question: 'What do I want to tell them?' The classic example is a subordinate, eager to impress the boss, who fills reports with accounts of how busy they have been. The boss, even busier, does not need a blow-by-blow account of the subordinate's day, but does need to know:

- What has been achieved (*not* how it was done)

- Are there any outstanding problems?

- If so, what is going to be done about these problems?

- Does the writer want any help from the boss with sorting the problems?

How much time does the reader have for my communication?

You won't know exactly, but make an estimate and plan the piece accordingly. Assume there is less time than you think.

Don't assume the reader will equate a document's length with its importance. People aren't that stupid. Length will prompt the thought, 'This had better be important,' but if the document starts looking like it's overblown, it will soon rack up contempt. Remember Mark Twain's famous comment: 'I'm sorry to write such a long letter: I didn't have time to write a short one.'

Keep your reader in mind as you write and as you rewrite. Remember our Golden Rule – every word should lead your reader forward. Not just any old reader, but yours . . .

Thinking 'reader'

- Who is going to read this?

  - imagine an 'archetype'

- Have I got credibility with this person?

- What is their level of technical knowledge?

- What do they need to know?

  - or, away from work, what would they like to know?

- How much time do they have to attend to me?

- Keep the reader in mind throughout the writing process.

Planning

Start with the basics. *What is your piece about?* What's its key message? Most short pieces by professional journalists make one point. Taking a (business) magazine at random from the shelves above my desk, I find pieces with the following messages:

- There are too many people telling business owners what they 'should' do.

- High-end retail businesses are similar to 'business-to-business' ones.

- It's harder to get stuff done than many people think.

- Do big-business bosses secretly despise their customers?

None of the pieces is earth-shattering, but they all make a point, elaborate on it a bit, then either restate it or revisit it in some new way in the light of the elaborations. The pieces work nicely because they are planned and focused.

Even large works can often be boiled down to simple, basic themes – it's the depth, breadth, integrity, thoroughness and originality of the themes' exploration that makes a great long piece of work. (One can, of course, take boiling-down too far. I like Woody Allen's joke: 'I've just speed-read *War and Peace*. It's about Russians.')

So, what is your piece about? In a couple of sentences, please.

Once you have established what you are writing about, the next question is, *What are you going to say about it?* Make a list of points you want to make.

What happens for me is that this list grows once I start answering another question – *How am I going to say it?* – and start doing some proper planning. Which leads nicely on to the topic of structure.

Structure

There are two basic structures – narrative and aspect-by-aspect.

Simple **narrative** is the best way of ensuring a piece flows. I believe we are born with an instinct for narrative – 'Tell me a story,' our children ask from a very early age. This happened; then that happened; then that happened. Beginning, middle and end.

If you are describing long, complex processes, think of how you can break these down into phases or stages – groups of naturally related actions that occur reasonably closely together in time. These will be the sections of the piece.

For example, the process of doing a commercial deal could be broken down into:

- Initial contact

- Testing how serious both sides are

- Producing an outline agreement

- Building trust

- Negotiating detail

- Last-minute problems

- Signing.

Clearly some sections may overlap in time – 'building trust', for example, is pretty much a continuous process – while others fit clearly into time-slots. Point this out to the reader. But you can still order them sequentially if you:

- Order them by starting time

- Explain where they overlap

- If the overlaps are complex, use a bar diagram to illustrate them.

The other basic structure for looking at a topic is **aspect-by-aspect**. A book on literary criticism could take a historical (narrative) view, or it could arrange its material this way: drama, poetry, novels, short stories, non-fiction (or any other way of subdividing the subject).

When planning to present material aspect-by-aspect, a 'mind-map' is hugely useful. Put the subject at the centre of the page, then imagine various aspects radiating out from it like spokes from a hub. For example, a piece for a local paper on a proposed bypass might look at the consequences for various groups of town residents: motorists, farmers, traders, shoppers, children getting to school etc. Each one of these would have a 'spoke' coming off the hub. The analogy between the mind-map and a bicycle wheel breaks down, of course, when spokes of the mind-map fork or multi-divide: 'The new bypass will have four main consequences for town traders . . .'

If you're stuck for spokes, remember Kipling's Elephant's Child, who said:

> I keep six honest serving-men
> (They taught me all I knew);
> Their names are What and Why and When
> And How and Where and Who.

If asked to write a piece on 'Thanksgiving Day', the Elephant's Child would produce a piece that told readers what it is, what the meaning of it is, on what day it's celebrated, what actually happens, where it's celebrated, and the sort of people who celebrate it.

When you come to turn the mind-map into a plan for a piece of writing, put the aspects in an order that readers will find useful. Unless otherwise instructed, they will assume that the first point you make is the most important one. Use this, or tell the reader that you are going to list the aspects in some other order, such as cost. Don't waste the opportunity to pass information to the reader by just placing things in random order.

A useful tool is the 'dialectic'. This isn't anything to do with Dalek-speak, fortunately, but a way of presenting arguments. It's been compared to tennis.

- Here's the standard view on the subject (the 'thesis').

- Now, here is the opposite argument (the 'antithesis') – or, more often and more interesting, here are some other opposing views.

- And my view (the 'synthesis') is . . .

Actually, most 'theses' have several antitheses, which is not what the founders of the dialectic believed. Work through them sequentially:

- Thesis

- Antithesis A

- Comments on Antithesis A

- Antithesis B

- Comments on Antithesis B

- Antithesis C

- Comments on Antithesis C

- (and so on . . .)

- My view.

Academic essays work well following this model, especially if the last section agrees with what the person marking the paper thinks.

Of course, you can embed one of the basic structures in the other. So the literary criticism book that divided topics into drama, poetry, novels, short stories and non-fiction could then deal with each of these historically (narrative embedded in aspect-by-aspect). Or the aspect-by-aspect treatment of specific issues can be embedded in a narrative: in the piece on the bypass, you could begin with some history (traffic growth since 1970, early protest groups etc.) up to the current moment. Then the middle section could deal aspect-by-aspect with the various issues shown in the mind-map, and finally a section could talk about the future.

A business report might follow the model below, which has a 'narrative' feel to it but is not just a simple story:

- Current problem

- Initial attempts at solving it, and why they failed

- Proposed new solution

- Implications of new solution for various parts of the business/other relevant parties

- Any objections, and how they will be met

- Specific actions required of individual people/departments

- Paint a picture of what things will be like when the new solution is put into practice successfully.

Once you have thought through your overall plan, you really are ready to get writing!

Planning your piece

- Theme
  - What's your piece about?
- Structure
  - Narrative

    Phases
  - Aspect-by-aspect

    Make a mind-map
  - Dialectic

    Work through the theses and antitheses.

9 Getting it done – the actual process of writing

You've laid out the basic plan for the piece – what it's about; what you're going to say about this topic. You know how you're going to structure your presentation of the material.

Go!

The process

Begin by writing a **'skeleton' outline**. For a long piece (and the advice that follows is essentially about writing long pieces), this should be about three to five pages of A4, or around 30 PowerPoint slides.

If you can, actually deliver this to an audience as a **talk**. If you can't find a real audience, try colleagues, family, the cat, the bathroom mirror . . . It's amazing how arguments can look fine on paper, but suddenly feel inadequate when spoken out loud.

If you do give the talk live, take note of any criticisms made. There are various possibilities:

- The critic is right – you're wrong.

- The critic is right, given their perspective, but this perspective isn't yours or your target audience's. For example, many of the points made in this book are not relevant to writing fiction, but a novelist who stood up and said that the points were 'wrong' would be foolish.

- The critic just has a different belief. On most subjects worth discussing, there are competing views. For example when I speak about entrepreneurship, I say that entrepreneurs are born not made – you have to be a certain type of person to endure the hassles and setbacks of starting a business. Other people don't agree, and believe that 'anyone can do it'. Rather than get bogged down in argument – both sides have ammunition for their views – I say, 'This is what I believe; other people disagree; make your own mind up,' and move on to the next topic.

- The critic is simply wrong.

Don't be swayed by critics without thinking which of the above categories they belong to.

Of course, you will also get comments from the floor of a more positive nature. 'I quite agree with what you said about x!' Accept the compliment with grace, and note any other observation the person makes. A positive comment is often a lead-in to something a person wants to say about their own experience – so let them tell the tale, and take note of it. Have a chat with them after the talk if you can. But at the same time, don't be swayed into thinking you now have the absolute truth! Think carefully about how these new comments illustrate or expand what you have to say, and build these new insights into the talk where relevant.

Having given the talk a few times, you should have a good idea about which parts of it are strong and where the weaknesses lie. It's time to go off and research the weaknesses. Read more; get googling; talk to experts (or, if you don't have access to experts, people with some experience of the topic). The end result of this should be a revised talk, and a **revised skeleton plan** that captures the essence of this talk.

Now it's time to do some real writing, as you 'flesh out' this skeleton, turning it into the **first full draft**.

The ideal way to write a first draft is to sit down with your revised skeleton plan, start writing, write to the end, then finish. Done.

In reality, different people draft differently. Some write, as recommended, straight through, beginning to end. Others pause midway and edit what has been written. I'm afraid I do the latter. I know that if I get to the end I can always redraft and rewrite, but somehow I need to have the feeling that I'm standing on something solid. If I don't feel that what I have written so far provides that solidity, I have to go back and rewrite. The danger of this approach is that you never get the draft finished; you are forever going back and tinkering. This is not good. Get that first draft done as quickly as you can!

In defence of pausing midway, then editing, priorities change as you write. Stuff that looked like it belonged in one section suddenly seems to belong somewhere else. Some more stuff you researched with great care still doesn't feel right, or begins to feel irrelevant. And, of course, if you have a complicated life, you may have to leave the drafting for a while, which means that when you come back to it, the only way to 'get back up to speed' is to start from the beginning.

In the end, I make a kind of compromise with myself. Early in the first drafting process, I'll go back and edit. But I give myself a deadline, after which I just run for the finishing tape.

This first draft then needs to be **reviewed**, ideally after some kind of break. One book on 'creative' writing recommended leaving the draft aside for three months – not a possibility for most of us. But at least give it a weekend. When you take it up again, print out a copy, pick up a blue or red pen, and go through it quickly, noting with a mark in the margin any bits that:

- read badly

- fail to make sense

- are boring, or

- don't say what you thought they would say.

Then, at the end of your read-through, close your eyes and try and think holistically. Overall, does the piece say:

- what you want to say

- in the way you want to say it

- to the people you are communicating with?

If not, what's the problem? Did the arguments flow logically? Were there steps missing? Was all the relevant information present? Note down your thoughts.

Now work through the piece again. Sort out the big problems first – what I call the **high-level rewrite**. Fill in any gaps in the argument. Is all the material in the right place? Often stuff is in the wrong section; it should either be in a section of its own or bundled in with another section. Move it around, and see how it now fits.

Don't be afraid to save various versions of your document. If you are planning a particularly audacious change – say, moving half a chapter to a new place – then rename it 'version 1.4'. If it turns out to have been a mistake, you can always sideline it and go back to working on version 1.3 (I find my computer won't save back-up copies of anything with a decimal point in, so I just number each version.

This actual sentence is being typed into version 10 of this book, but that does not mean I have written ten discrete, totally different versions of it! If I could use decimal points, it would probably be about version 3.2, the second edit of the third draft.)

When you feel that the logic of the piece now works, it's time to get the writing better: the **low-level rewrite**. Remember: 'Every word should lead your reader forward.'

You will find that every piece of writing is an ecosystem. Changing one piece of text always has 'knock-on' effects somewhere else. Never underestimate these. In your high-level rewrite, if you move a chunk of text from point A, early in the piece, to point C, later in the piece, you must be sure that there isn't some writing somewhere in between (at point B, for example) that assumes knowledge of what you originally said at A but now don't say till C. Conversely, if you move some text from C to A, is there something at B that was originally fresh and new but now repeats what you are now saying at A? In the low-level rewrite, if you substitute one word for another, you can bet that word will crop up in the next paragraph, so you suddenly have a repetition.

One of the most difficult tasks in revising is taking out material, especially if you put a lot of effort into it, or, hardest of all, if it is well-written, with a particular image or turn of phrase that you are proud of. Sadly, if the material is misleading, irrelevant or repetitious, it has to go. By all means save it as a separate file. My guess is that once it has been saved, you will never look at it again, but at least your gem has been preserved.

When you have made all the necessary changes, you effectively have a **second full draft**. As with the first one, leave it for a bit, then revisit. Hopefully, it will be much tighter, better focused and will read better than your first version.

If you have time, repeat the revisiting and revising process.

If you want to, now is also the time to ask **outsiders** to have a look. I stress the 'if you want to', as you have every right to say, 'No, I don't want people butting in. I've done my research; I know what I'm saying.' Other writers like the security of an objective comment at this point.

The kind of outsider you want is a subject-matter expert. You don't want amateur critics making comments about your style – if you've read this book and worked at your writing, you're probably a better writer than they are – but you might need the reassurance that you really have covered the topic and not made any howlers.

In practice, some outsiders will enthusiastically agree to read your piece, then you'll never hear from them again. Others will provide helpful input. 'I especially liked the bit about x,' is both nice to hear and helpful in pinpointing the strengths of your document – necessary if you are intending to sell or promote it in some way. Some others will just point out that you've made a typo on page 136.

In all cases, thank outsiders for their time in looking at the document and for any input that they have provided. Buy them lunch or a bottle of nice wine. Over time, you will develop a 'stable' of outsiders whom you know and trust to take time to look at your work and to make the right sorts of comments. Work only with these people – life is much easier that way.

You should now have the confidence to regard the document as up to the job. Great.

I recommend one last read-through with a coloured pen to check small errors; then it's finished. By amending your second draft you have produced, by definition, a **third and final draft**. And that should be that. Remind yourself of the old advice, 'Perfect is the enemy of done.' A finished piece that says 90 per cent of what needs saying, and does so adequately well, is better than a masterpiece that nobody ever gets to read because the author is always tinkering with it in pursuit of perfection.

Drafting

- Skeleton outline:

  - 3–5 pages of A4

  - 30 PowerPoint slides

- Talk

- Revised skeleton

- First full draft

  - Get it done!

  - Let it rest

- Second full draft

  - Review and revise

  - High-level rewrite

  - Low-level rewrite

  - Revise once more if you have time

- Outsiders' views

  - Only if you want to

- Third and final draft

  - A final read-through for small errors

  - 'Perfect is the enemy of done'.

The section above is aimed at people writing long works. You can't go through this rigmarole for a short memorandum or article, but do follow a truncated version of it:

- What is the piece about and what do you want to say about this?

- Plan.

- Write a first draft.

- Put this aside, if only for a night, then come back to it. Professional journalists, up against deadlines, will often write their piece, do a quick read-through, make a few changes then send it off. Fine: they are professionals. For everyone else, a chance to 'revisit and revise' is of huge value.

Presentation

Your work now needs to be presented in as readable and attractive a way as possible – don't waste all the effort of good writing by producing a document that is unreadable, or even just 'reader-unfriendly'. For essays and Ph.D.s, your tutor will tell you what the house rules are (they will be quite simple, and you can prepare the document yourself). For documents with any commercial importance, get them set and printed professionally. But many small documents don't fall into either of the above categories – there are no 'house rules'; you can't afford to get a pro to design them; you have to do them yourself.

Fine. It's creative; it's not difficult; it's fun. Here are some basic points:

Space

The biggest single mistake people make is to cram their documents too full of text. If you have a lot to say, allow it to 'breathe' by using two pages rather than one. Professional designers use lots of 'white space'. Look at the ads in newspapers – large areas of this highly expensive space are taken up by . . . nothing.

The reason is, of course, to focus the reader's attention on a few crucial points.

For a simple document, make sure you:

- Have decent-sized margins to both the left and the right of the text.

- Have proper spacing between lines (the technical term for this is 'leading'). One-and-a-half or double, not single. Lines with one space between them look all bunched up, especially if there are loads of them on a page. They are harder to read: we read by recognising the shapes of words, and this is much more difficult if lines are close together. Also, the eye can easily wander off one line of text on to another. I often see documents formatted in this style, and it doesn't do the writer any favours.

- In writing non-fiction, I like to leave blank lines between each paragraph. (This doesn't work in fiction writing, where there's dialogue, so I don't have blank lines between paragraphs but indent the start of each paragraph.)

- Leave space at the top and bottom of the text. Especially at the beginning.

- In a very brief document with less than one full page of material, make sure the page is balanced, rather than having a whole lot of text at the top and a lot of white space at the bottom. Move the text towards the middle. Increase the margins by making the text 'box' narrower. Increase the 'spacing' to 'double'. Move the heading away from the text and increase its font size. Above all, use your aesthetic judgement. Zoom out to look at the whole page. Does it look nice or ugly?

Fonts

Please use standard, readable typefaces (or 'fonts'). There are basically three types:

- Those with 'serifs'. A serif is a tiny embellishment to the basic letter shape that makes the letter easier to recognise. This, of course, makes text easier to read, and thus helps the brain get into a 'flow' state, so use these for your basic text. Times New Roman is the classic one.

- Fonts without serifs, known as sans-serif. Sans-serif fonts like Helvetica and Arial are often used in headings, to create variety when the main text is in a serif font – though I use Times New Roman both for headings and main text, and it looks fine to me! Some people believe that sans-serif fonts are easier to read off computer screens, which is why the default font for the emails you receive is Arial. Incidentally, years ago, the *Guardian* ran a travel supplement on an idyllic holiday island, showing things like its annual spaghetti harvest. It appeared on 1 April, and the island was called San Serif.

- Novelty fonts. These are to be avoided in any serious communication, and to be used sparingly in humorous ones. If you must use these, keep them to headings and perhaps a wacky first letter of a piece. The problem is quite simple: they are hell to read.

Different fonts work best in different sizes (also called 'points'). I find 11- or 12-point Times New Roman produces a nice, readable page; 10-point is a bit small, and 14 too clumsy.

Headings

Think through your 'hierarchy of headings'.

A short, one-page document might have the main heading in 14-point bold and the rest of the text in 12- or 11-point. Don't make the heading much, much larger, the way tabloid papers do with their headline. It's a bit like shouting at people; two or three points bigger is quite enough.

The alternative is to have no headings and let readers find their own way (which they won't), or to label every paragraph and bullet with numbers, like 9.1.1.2 (= section 9, sub-section 1, paragraph 1, bullet point 2). The latter works well in legal contracts, which are not designed to be easily read but which need to be easily referenced, but it's ugly and off-putting anywhere else.

Justification

This means having straight lines at both the left and right margins of the text. All text should be 'left-hand justified', which means a nice straight line down the left-hand side of the text. Proper books have nice straight lines left and right, which creates authoritative-looking blocks of text.

The drawback to this is that because you've had to fit the text into what is effectively a box, you end up with the spacing between words being different on different lines – some lines look all bunched up, others look all stretched out, which is tiring on the eye. Professionally printed books get round this by various subtle techniques, including hyphenating words at line-ends to keep a consistent average number of letters (or spaces or punctuation marks) per line. You haven't the time to do this (or the skill: typesetters know where to hyphenate a word to stop it looking silly). I recommend that if you're preparing a document yourself, left-hand justify only.

There's a special moment when you see *your* piece properly presented for the first time. Enjoy that feeling – it will soon be replaced by another one. The moment it is finished, printed and ready to be sent out into the world, you will find flaws in it. Don't be upset by this: it happens to all writers (and other types of artist. The apocryphal story is told of various great artists – Monet, Whistler – that they sneaked back into galleries to 'improve' their works). Take a deep breath; admit you're not perfect; allow yourself to feel proud, of a job done well and professionally.

I'd like to conclude this chapter with some comments on the process of working with other people on writing.

Writing as a group or pair

Many documents are written by **groups** of people. Someone needs to be in charge, and have the role of editor. This can be a demanding job. This person needs:

• to be a good writer

• to have adequate technical knowledge of the subject

• diplomacy

- firmness

- the ability to inspire and motivate the rest of the team.

The team need to agree the basic points, then brainstorm the mind-map (and any pruning of the mind-map). The team leader should then draw up the skeleton outline, which should be circulated and agreed. Then the leader must allocate sections to relevant people, who then go off and write first drafts by agreed dates. The leader should then gather these, chasing any late submitters, and turn them all into a first full draft of the document. This will almost undoubtedly involve some editing. Contributors will inevitably complain about this: the leader should listen carefully, in case there is some necessary technical subtlety that has been edited out. But in the end, 'the editor's decision is final'.

This first full draft should be circulated, and the team should meet to discuss. Where are the 'holes'? Usually it's obvious who the right person to fill the holes is, but if not, the team leader must decide.

Any rewriting is submitted to the leader, who then produces a second draft, which is circulated. At this point, any objections or problems should be minor ones. A final meeting, and the leader goes away, makes any changes he or she thinks fit, then circulates the document to all contributors for them to 'sign off'.

This model is rather undemocratic, but pieces written by groups with no one in charge lack authority. Readers want to know who is talking to them. (As screenplay guru Robert McKee points out, the words *author* and *authority* have the same root.) If a document is an agglomeration of contributions by diverse individuals, keep it in sections and attribute each section to an author.

On a more practical level, projects with no leader at best tend to take ages, at worst never get completed.

Smaller joint documents can be passed round electronically and have attributed comments left on them. Fine; but, as always, someone must be responsible for the end product, and that someone must have the final say in which changes are accepted and which rejected.

Maybe this will change with the rise of entities like Wikipedia, an online encyclopaedia written by anonymous contributors who just send stuff in. But even Wikipedia has people moderating the process to keep out ranters, ideologically motivated misinformation or people who just get stuff wrong.

It's quite common to write as a **pair** – a subject-matter expert and a professional writer. Hopefully, after reading this book, subject-matter experts will be better at communicating their knowledge, but if you are still doubtful, get a professional writer.

There are three keys to making this relationship work:

- Find someone you like.

- Find someone who already has some knowledge of, and, more important, an interest in, your subject.

- Be clear from the outset about the nature and details of your co-operation.

The first two points are pretty self-explanatory. On the third, I work in one of two ways with subject-matter experts. One is to work quite closely, helping them plan the book, then getting regular 'brain-dumps' from them – in person, not via email or post or even telephone – which I then go away and write up, and which they subsequently review. The other way is simply to be an editor: the expert provides a text and I rewrite it, as little as possible but as much as is necessary. The person-to-person method is one I use for books; the more distant, editorial method is fine for short pieces (especially ones where there's little money going, so nobody can afford long debriefs and discussions).

You will need to be clear from the outset about issues such as:

- *Confidentiality*. The writer must agree to this.

- *Time and money*. The writer must be paid. The expert is getting exposure: a good book is a wonderful brochure and will do wonders for their career. The expert should pay for this. It needs to be agreed in advance how much time the writer is to spend, and what the reward will be.

- *Attribution*. Will the piece be 'ghosted' (just the expert's name on the cover, with a 'thank you' in the foreword) or fully co-authored? In between these extremes are options such as listing the writer as 'editor' or putting them on the cover but in a clearly subordinate position ('by Fred Bloggs with Joanna Soap').

- *Ownership*. Co-authored works should, rather obviously, be the copyright of both authors. Ghosted stuff should belong to the expert, as it's their intellectual property. If the 'expert' is actually not an expert on anything at all but just a celebrity, the copyright will probably belong to the publishers, which is fair as they will no doubt have paid a fortune to secure the rights.

As with any project, team authorship – group and pair – needs to be managed, and its progress compared against clear 'milestones': 'We want to be on chapter four by January . . .'

Team authorship is not easy, but can work when the above rules are followed.

10 Specific writing situations – some hints

Email

Email is probably the most common form of written communication now. When it was first being widely used, email was thought of as a kind of instant letter, but now it has developed its own characteristics, distinct from phone conversations or letters.

EMAIL	PHONE	LETTER
Informal	Informal	Formal
Written	Verbal	Written
Arrives quickly, but may not be read or answered at once	Instant	Takes time to arrive
Keep it brief!	Can be a nice long chat	Can be longer
Easy to copy to many people	One-to-one	Usually one-to-one
Waits to be read	Intrusive – answer me now!	Waits to be read
Poor security	Poor security	Security better

If it's like any pre-existing medium, email is like the postcard.

Email is best used for simple things – a question, an answer to a question. Even with longer emails, try and fit them on to the page that appears when you click them open, which allows for about 20 lines of text.

How should emails be written? The answer, in my view, is: correctly. There's no excuse for bad grammar or punctuation. There's no excuse for failure to think through and marshal material. Particularly, there's no excuse for rubbish spelling, as most email systems have a spellchecker. I do accept that the level of style can be a bit lower – for example one can get away with more repeated words – but email is not an excuse for reverting to pre-literate English, especially if you are writing in a business context. By all means dash off an answer to a quick 'question' email – *Yes, see you at the Rose and Crown, 12.30* – but anything longer requires thought.

Where an email has serious content with long-term consequences, I suggest working on it as a Word document, then 'pasting' it into the email. Having done this, reread it and allow for small changes – sometimes phrases that sound fine in the Word document look a bit stiff and formal when ready to be sent off as email.

And, of course, remember the adage, 'Email in haste, repent at leisure'! It's very easy to bash out an email when in a powerful but fleeting mood and fire it off in the heat of the moment to whoever has got you into this mood. Unwise. Think before you click. Or, better still, store it in the draft folder and don't send it till the next morning.

Whatever kind of email you are writing, layout is important – reading from a screen is harder than reading from paper. Use short paragraphs and leave blank lines between them. At the same time, don't go in for fancy formatting, as some recipients' machines can't handle this. By all means 'upgrade' emails to html, which allows you to use italics and put the other person's email replies in blue if replying paragraph by paragraph (this sounds 'techie', but is actually very simple: the computer will ask you if you want to 'switch to html' if you click on an icon that the other formats can't handle), but otherwise keep the formatting simple.

There's a debate about how to begin emails. *Dear* — sounds a bit formal; *Hi* — sounds a bit casual; just the person's name sounds a bit peremptory. With people I don't know I use *Dear* —. With people I know, I've slipped into the habit of using '*Hi* —', which is fine as long as the email is friendly rather than critical (if it's critical, I tend to revert to 'Dear —'). In the end, you have to work out what suits you.

The same goes for signing off. Letters had nice clear rules; email hasn't. Yet.

The 'subject' box is important, especially if you are emailing people you don't know, as this is what they will see before deciding to open it. If you are writing on a personal recommendation, mention that person in the subject box. If not, then pick out what is it about your email that will be of interest to them.

There is quite a lot of material around about email etiquette, all of it largely agreed:

- Don't use capitals or !!!

- Don't attach documents unless requested to.

- Stay in the 'thread' (in other words, click 'Reply' not 'New' when answering someone's email, which will mean that all the previous correspondence gets sent back with your reply).

- Don't send on chain letters.

- Answer quickly – within 24 hours . . .

- . . . but don't expect instant replies: if a message is really urgent, get on the phone.

- Do answer all the questions asked in an email (that sounds obvious, but lots of people don't do that, and it's infuriating). If you don't know the answer now, but will do in the future, say so, and give a time by which the recipient can expect an answer. Contact the recipient again when that time is up.

- Don't overuse the red 'urgent' exclamation mark. The other day, I got an 'urgent' email announcing an event in three months' time. I was not impressed.

- Don't spam, or semi-spam. Write emails to actual people.

- If, for some reason, you do get 'flamed' (sent an abusive email) by someone, don't get into an argument. If, in retrospect, you realise you did something wrong and deserved it, apologise. But if the flamer is just looking for a fight, ignore them; they'll go away and annoy somebody else.

Memoranda

'Memos' are often sent via email, but deserve a brief mention on their own. As with emails, they should be brief and to the point. Head them with the basics: from, to, date, subject. For the actual text, this three-section model covers most memos:

- Problem

- Solution

- Specific action(s). What do you want the recipient to do? What are you intending to do or what have you done?

Instructions

The number one rule for instructions is to 'think reader'. Ideally, you should talk to users and find out which aspects they find, or found, difficult. If a machine/piece of software/procedure is totally new, let potential users try it. Watch what they do, talk with them as they do it, and debrief afterwards.

If this is not possible, think hard about 'segmenting'. What sort of person will be following the instructions? What level of technical knowledge will they have? The answer to the last question is usually 'less than you think'. If in doubt, imagine your instructions being read by a person who is of average intelligence but who has no technical knowledge at all.

Here are ten key points for creating good instructions:

- Take the user step by step through all the main procedures. If the process is at all interactive – e.g. with a machine – don't just say what the user should do, but say what the machine will do in response. *Turn machine on. The power light (see diagram 3) should go on.*

- Again, for a machine, list, and ideally show in a picture, all the component parts and describe what they do.

- For software, show the main screens that the user will see.

- List common user mistakes.

- Have a 'troubleshooting' section. *If x doesn't work, this is usually because of one of three things: either a) . . .*

- For a long set of instructions, list contents at the front and a thorough index at the back.

- If you send someone somewhere with instructions (e.g. from one page of a website to another), make sure those instructions can be carried out. It's infuriating to be told, *Click here, then click on the X section of the new page*, to find that when you get to the new page, there's no X section in sight. Computer nerds, of course, know that the icon with a Y on it is also known as an X, or that if you right click on the Z button you get X. The rest of us don't know that, and don't care: we just want to use the site.

- Don't be afraid to 'over-explain'. Users will just skip the bits they already know.

- Use imperatives – *Open the lid* – rather than passives – *The lid should be opened.*

- Remember that technical vocabulary doesn't just mean nouns. Will the user understand all the verbs and adjectives you use?

Advertisements

Clearly, doing huge advertisements for corporate campaigns is an art best left to professionals, but many of us have to write ads of some kind, and, actually, the basic form we should use is the same as the one underlying the professionals' work. Any ad is a kind of process, taking the reader through a journey which begins with them noticing the ad and ends with them taking the action you want them to. (Those incredibly glossy TV car ads don't end up with any call to 'action' – but they are an exception.)

This journey is often boiled down into the formula AIDA:

- Attention

- Interest

- Desire

- Action.

I've seen various other versions, usually variations on this, but AIDA is the only one I can remember, probably because it's a real word (complete with elephants) rather than just an agglomeration of letters.

Attention is usually drawn by a picture or a simple heading in large print. The picture or heading should be relevant. We all groan at ads that say SEX in big letters, then go on, *Now we've got your attention, we'd like to talk about our new line in organic pasta . . .*

Interest is aroused by readers perceiving that the ad relates to them and their interests in a specific way. Best of all, the ad relates to a problem they currently have. (A serial entrepreneur I met in America said that when considering a new business idea, he asked the simple question: 'Where's the pain?') Otherwise, does it relate to something they would like to have, be or do?

Desire means, obviously, that readers are no longer just interested by, but actually want, your 'offer' (whatever you are advertising). Getting them to this state involves at least three steps (which is where the complications to the AIDA acronym come in). You must:

- explain how your offer solves their problem/satisfies their want

- then convince them that it will work

- then convince them that it will work *for them.*

You may also have to convince them that they can afford it (or, rather, that your offer represents *value*: it may cost £x, but will be worth a lot more than that to them). After this, they should be eager to buy.

Action is the opportunity to do something about it, right now. *Here's a form to fill in; ring this number* etc.

Sales letters

These should be written with the same AIDA process in mind.

There are two types of sales letter. One is a specific one to people with whom you are acquainted (i.e. whom you have met, but don't know that well). The key obstacle to overcome here is to remind them of that acquaintance. Once they say, 'Oh, yes, I remember,' then you have credibility and can get on with the 'interest, desire, action' stuff.

For letters to people unknown to you – for example, people selected from mailing lists – the key is in the 'headline', that underlined bit across the top of the text. This must speak to the reader – or the letter goes in the bin.

Take time crafting the headline. Don't just go with the first idea you think of; try various alternatives. Get other people to look at the various versions and see which one works for them.

Remember the rule: Think 'reader'.

Reports

I covered the basics of a good report in the section on structure – see page 120 for the model structure I suggested. Clearly not every report fits this model, but with a little intelligent tinkering many reports will benefit from this structure.

Reports also need 'topping and tailing' – topping with a powerful summary, and tailing with an index, so readers can refer back to sections with ease and confidence, and sometimes also references.

Many people say that the **summary** is the most important part of a report. It is certainly the most read part – so you must get all your main points into it. Some of you might object that this takes the interest out of the rest of it, a bit like prefacing a whodunnit by saying, *The butler did it; and the giveaway clue is that the colonel thought he heard a gun being fired, but actually it was the vicar's car backfiring.* But many people just read the summary. The job of the report is to back up the conclusions presented in the summary with detailed arguments, facts and figures.

The summary must be in plain language, and should only be one page long. It must cover:

• The problem

• Your recommended solution

• The main implications of that solution (cost, time etc.).

The summary is sometimes called an 'executive summary'. The word 'executive' has absolutely no meaning here, other than to make the summary sound important – presumably, high-flying executives will read it, while other, less important people, such as dustmen, housewives or people who write books on English, won't. In other words, the term is just another piece of business pomposity.

Indexing is largely a matter of thoroughness. When I index books, I look for the one place where a topic is discussed in greatest depth, and send readers to that page. If you want to cite all the pages where a topic is mentioned, help the reader by putting the site of the main discussion in bold.

Referencing is often important in reports – those readers who get beyond the summary may well want to check your facts and/or quotes, so provide references for them to do so. As you research, keep notes on where you get each major piece of information or quote from – it's infuriating having a key piece of info to hand, but, having forgotten where you got it from, wasting ages looking back through your sources to find out. (Don't fool yourself that you'll remember. If you're at all like me, you won't.)

If you want to use full academic-style referencing, it follows this pattern:

> Author(s), *Title of Work* (Place of origin: publisher, date of publication)

So

> West, C, *My Great Test Career for England* (London: Cricketing Press, 2007)

(Sadly, this refers to a work of fiction.)

Less formally, just say something like:

> Source: C West, *My Great Test Career for England.*

This should be enough to direct the reader to the right place.

Business plans

These are similar to reports, in that the summary is by far the most important section, and the rest of the plan is simply back-up for that magic first page. (Actually, if you are showing your plan to people outside the company, the first pages have to be legalistic stuff, but readers usually ignore this and go straight for the summary.)

There are plenty of model business plans available, free, on the internet. Use one as a template, and remember to avoid managementese in your writing!

Business letters

The basic rules of good writing matter hugely here. Use ordinary, not pompous words. Be ruthless in checking for, and removing, ambiguity – both actual and potential, remember.

Ideally, your letter should fit on to a page.

The old rules for ending letters were:

- If you addressed the letter to an individual, *Dear Ms Smith*, you ended *Yours sincerely*.

- If you addressed the letter *Dear Sir/Madam*, then you ended *Yours faithfully*.

That usage seems to be dying out, which is a bit of a shame, as the rule, once understood, made things easy. Now, my computer tells me to end, *Yours truly*, which I find pretty naff. I stick to the old rules.

General interest pieces

Remember the question 'What's the piece about?' Well-known people can get away with a series of rambling thoughts on life, the universe and everything; the rest of us can't, and need to be saying something specific to merit taking up readers' time and attention.

Listen to Radio 4's *From Our Own Correspondent* for a master-class in writing this kind of piece. The correspondents almost always start by painting a very specific picture – describing a person or an event. This then leads into the topic to be discussed. At the end of the piece, they 'pay off' the intro by returning to it and looking at it in the light of what has been talked about in between.

Remember to find out from the medium where your piece will appear how many words they want – and stick to that figure.

Web pages

People read web copy more slowly than they do paper copy, but they are also more impatient. As a result, you have to grab the site-visitor's attention quickly and make sure that you keep it. But this book has been all about doing just that, so if you have taken all my points on board, you will be a good web writer. Even if you've only taken on the Golden Rule ('every word should lead your reader forward') you'll be ahead of many web writers.

A few specialist web points are worth noting, however:

- Research shows that many readers don't scroll, so get all your information on to one screen. (I break this rule on my own site, but most visitors are keen readers, who probably will scroll.)

- Every page should have a 'headline', to grab the attention of the click-happy surfer. These should be simple and factual, not clever.

- As with email, use short sentences and short paragraphs. Have space between the paragraphs.

- Use highlighted words – but don't overload your text with them. One or two per paragraph is ideal. Note: hyperlinks (those blue underlined words you click on that take you automatically to another page) can double as highlighted words.

- Use headings.

- Use bullet points.

- Use sans-serif typefaces.

The nature of hyperlinks has altered the way pieces of writing are structured on the web. A ten-page document should be boiled down to a one-page summary, with hyperlinks on each main aspect so that readers who want to investigate that aspect more deeply can click and be taken to a secondary, specialist page.

You will sometimes see long, traditionally structured pieces such as essays and reports online – not on front pages, but in archives that you have to click to reach. These are largely there to be downloaded. If you are including such material on a site, provide a simple summary and a 'printer-friendly version'.

PowerPoint slides

As with all communication, keep these simple. The ideal PowerPoint slide has a heading and three or four bulleted points. Nothing more. I've sat though some appalling presentations that were just printed pages transferred to a slide. There's no way people sitting in a semi-dark room can read these off a screen – give them out as handouts. Even worse are illegible slides in arty fonts. Stop showing off and have more consideration for your audience!

Conclusion: the nine commandments

Simplicity has been an underlying theme of this book, so I would like to end it with 'nine commandments' that, I hope, sum up what I have been saying. (I've kept it to nine: the original ten was a set of instructions about how to live, while I am only talking about how to write – important, but not *that* important!)

- Think 'reader'.

- Plan.

- The Golden Rule: every word should lead your reader forward.

- Seek out, and eliminate, all ambiguity, actual or potential.

- In complex sentences, get subject, verb, object down as quickly as possible.

- Use variety and balance.

- Give your paragraphs both unity and flow.

- Clarity, clarity, clarity.

- Remember – you are being creative.

I'd like to add a few thoughts on the last two commandments:

Clarity

Above all else, good non-fiction writing is clear writing. Think of a beautiful pool – in a mountain stream, or among rocks at the seashore – of clear, unpolluted water, where you can see all the life in it and every detail of the sides and bottom. Let your writing be as limpid and inviting as that.

Don't be fooled by people who say such writing is simplistic. It is not; it is very hard to accomplish, and a fine achievement if you do.

And don't be fooled by people who regard such writing as an optional extra, as a kind of pleasant but non-essential ornament. Clear writing and clear thinking are inextricably linked. Nobel laureate (1976) Milton Friedman wrote:

> *People often excuse bad writing by saying that they know what they mean, and simply have difficulty expressing it. That is nonsense. If you cannot state a proposition clearly and unambiguously, you do not understand it.*

Just think of that rockpool and strive for clarity.

This is creative!

There is currently a proliferation of university (and other) courses in 'creative writing', by which the course-givers mean fiction, drama or poetry. Don't be fooled into thinking that other kinds of writing are not creative. Writing good, clear, informative, enjoyable non-fiction prose is a highly creative activity, and one any practitioner can be as proud of as any novelist, playwright or poet.

I hope you will enjoy the journey of becoming a better non-fiction writer. It is potentially never-ending – words have been my profession for twenty years, and I'm still learning and enjoying learning. The pleasure takes many forms. It lies in the act of writing itself. It lies in the pride of doing a good job – in writing something then reading it back and thinking, 'Yes, I've done justice to myself, to the subject and to my readers.' It lies in my ever-increasing ability to appreciate good writing in other people. And it lies in being part of a community of people committed to high standards in what we do.

Anyone can belong to this community if they care about their writing. You've read this book. You're planning to act on what it says. Welcome aboard!

Quick Reference: recommended reads

My two favourite 'how to' books on writing good clear English are:

- Phythian, B A *Correct English* London: Teach Yourself, 1992. All the basics of grammar, punctuation etc. are presented in a friendly and accessible fashion. The book has recently been revamped, and is, in my view, not as good as it was before (though it's still useful) – keep your eyes open for an older edition.

- Williams, J M *Style: The Basics of Clarity and Grace* Essex: Longman, 2005. Excellent on balance and on keeping unity and flow in paragraphs.

I also continue to find this one incredibly (and slightly embarrassingly, as I ought to know these things) useful:

- Room, A *Hutchinson Pocket Dictionary of Confusable Words* Abingdon: Helicon, 1999.

Other useful handbooks are:

- Strunk, W and White, E B *The Elements of Style* Essex: Longman, 1999. A deserved classic.

- Cutts, M *Oxford Guide to Plain English* Oxford: Oxford University Press, 2007

- Law, J *The Language Toolkit* Oxford: Oxford University Press, 2002. (Come on, Light Blues – where are you?)

On punctuation:

- Curtis, S *Perfect Punctuation* London: Random House, 2007. Another title in the *Perfect* series, giving an accessible and detailed look at punctuation.

- Truss, L *Eats, Shoots and Leaves* London: Profile, 2007. Polemical and fun, but with good instructional content too. She goes into the history of punctuation marks, as well as their current use.

- Carey, G V *Mind the Stop* Cambridge: Cambridge University Press, 1971.

And of course, those two classics:

- Burchfield, R W *Fowler's Modern English Usage 3rd Edition* Oxford: Oxford University Press, 2004.

- Gowers, E *The Complete Plain Words* Boston: David R. Godine, 2004.

To which I would add another classic:

- Ayto, J *Brewer's Dictionary of Phrase and Fable 17th Edition* London: Cassell, 2007 – which isn't really a how-to book, but if you love words you'll just get lost in this.

Standing outside one's own language and looking in can be refreshing. The Dutch are the best users of English around (better than a lot of English!), and you'll find *Perfect Your English the Easy Way* by WH Ballin clear, unstuffy and useful – if you can find it, that is, as it's published in Holland, by a company called Prisma.

Finally, there are many good places to go online for information. The best thing to do is just put 'commas' (or whatever you want to know about) in Google and see what comes up.

- Wikipedia can be relied on for good stuff (on everything and anything!).

- 'The Guide to Punctuation', by Larry Trask, on Sussex University's 'Informatics' site is excellent. (Students – there's more information on formal academic referencing here, especially if you are studying those eminent academics Curtis, Roberts, Lumley and Scacchi.)

- The KryssTal site I ended up on when looking into word origins has all sorts of useful information on language (plus some political stuff which represents the site authors' own views!).

No doubt there are many more places to go on the web: find your own favourites.

However handy all of the above are – and they are handy, believe me – nothing beats reading the work of the great non-fiction prose writers. If you go to uni to study English Literature, you are taught about the existence of a 'canon' of great works of fiction, the undoubted masterpieces that all properly read people should know. Exactly what's in this canon keeps changing, but old favourites like Shakespeare, Austen, Dickens, Eliot, Joyce and so on remain at its heart. There is no equivalent canon in non-fiction writing, which I find odd.

I'm not sure the list below constitutes a canon – I've kept it down to five writers, so it's more of a musket. And it's strictly about expression: a true canon of non-fiction would also contain the great reshapers of the intellectual landscape like Charles Darwin or

Mary Wollstonecraft, while the list below is more about great users of the language. Read these; enjoy reading them; see how it's done!

- The Bible, in the original King James version. For both musicality and precision in choice of words, this cannot be beaten. Usually books as beautiful and compelling as this are written by one individual, but this was the work of teams of scholars (though much of the credit must go to an earlier translator of the Bible, William Tyndale, on whose text this was based).

- *The Decline and Fall of the Roman Empire* by Edward Gibbon. I've already talked about the master of balance, so won't go on about him again here. Just read him!

- *Inside the Whale and Other Essays* by George Orwell. Orwell understood the link between clarity of expression and political liberty (and between jargon and tyranny) better than anyone. He also put this into practice with these marvellous essays that are both rockpool-clear and full of humanity.

- *Never Give In! The Best of Winston Churchill's Speeches.* Words that saved the world.

Work with the author

If you have enjoyed this book and found it useful, do get in touch with me via my website (authors spend far too much time sitting alone at computers, and like to hear from their readers).

I also teach writing. If you are an organisation wishing to improve your communication, internal and external, I run courses. These can be tailored to your needs and the time you have available (a day course is probably best, though a ninety-minute blitz can be remarkably effective). I am also a writing coach to individuals.

I am always updating my website, www.chriswest.info. Do visit and see what's new.

Best wishes,

Chris West

Perfect Punctuation

Stephen Curtis

All you need to get it right first time

- Do you find punctuation a bit confusing?
- Are you worried that your written English might show you up?
- Do you want a simple way to brush up your skills?

Perfect Punctuation is an invaluable guide to mastering punctuation marks and improving your writing. Covering everything from semi-colons to inverted commas, it gives step-by-step guidance on how to use each mark and how to avoid common mistakes. With helpful examples of correct and incorrect usage and exercises that enable you to practise what you've learned, *Perfect Punctuation* has everything you need to ensure that you never make a mistake again.

BOOKS

Perfect CV

Max Eggert

All you need to get it right first time

- Are you determined to succeed in your job search?
- Do you need guidance on how to make a great first impression?
- Do you want to make sure your CV stands out?

Bestselling *Perfect CV* is essential reading for anyone who's applying for jobs. Written by a leading HR professional with years of experience, it explains what recruiters are looking for, gives practical advice about how to show yourself in your best light, and provides real-life examples to help you improve your CV. Whether you're a graduate looking to take the first step on the career ladder, or you're planning an all-important job change, *Perfect CV* will help you stand out from the competition.

BOOKS

Perfect Interview

Max Eggert

All you need to get it right first time

- Are you determined to succeed in your job search?
- Do you want to make sure you have the edge on the other candidates?
- Do you want to find out what interviewers are *really* looking for?

Perfect Interview is an invaluable guide for anyone who's applying for jobs. Written by a leading HR professional with years of experience in the field, it explains how interviews are constructed, gives practical advice about how to show yourself in your best light, and provides real-life examples to help you practise at home. Whether you're a graduate looking to take the first step on the career ladder, or you're planning an all-important job change, *Perfect Interview* will help you stand out from the competition.

BOOKS

Perfect Personality Profiles

Helen Baron

All you need to get it right first time

- Have you been asked to complete a personality question-naire?
- Do you need guidance on the sorts of questions you'll be asked?
- Do you want to make sure you show yourself in your best light?

Perfect Personality Profiles is essential reading for anyone who needs to find out more about psychometric profiling. Including everything from helpful pointers on how to get ready to professionally constructed sample questions for you to try out at home, it walks you through every aspect of preparing for a test. Whether you're a graduate looking to take the first step on the career ladder, or you're planning an all-important job change, *Perfect Personality Profiles* has everything you need to make sure you stand out from the competition.

BOOKS

Perfect Psychometric Test Results

Joanna Moutafi and Ian Newcombe

All you need to get it right first time

- Have you been asked to sit a psychometric test?
- Do you want guidance on the sorts of questions you'll be asked?
- Do you want to make sure you perform to the best of your abilities?

Perfect Psychometric Test Results is an essential guide for anyone who wants to secure their ideal job. Written by a team from Kenexa, one of the UK's leading compilers of psychometric tests, it explains how each test works, gives helpful pointers on how to get ready, and provides professionally constructed sample questions for you to try out at home. It also contains an in-depth section on online testing – the route that more and more recruiters are choosing to take. Whether you're a graduate looking to take the first step on the career ladder, or you're planning an all-important job change, *Perfect Psychometric Test Results* has everything you need to make sure you stand out from the competition.

BOOKS

Perfect Pub Quiz

David Pickering

All you need to stage a great quiz

- Who invented the cat-flap?
- Which is the largest island in the world?
- What is tofu made of?

Perfect Pub Quiz is the ideal companion for all general knowledge nuts. Whether you're organising a quiz night in your local or you simply want to get in a bit of practice on tricky subjects, *Perfect Pub Quiz* has all the questions and answers. With topics ranging from the Roman Empire to *Little Britain* and from the Ryder Cup to Alex Rider, this easy-to-use quiz book will tax your brain and provide hours of fun.

BOOKS

Perfect Babies' Names

Rosalind Fergusson

All you need to choose the ideal name

- Do you want help finding the perfect name?
- Are you unsure whether to go for something traditional or something more unusual?
- Do you want to know a bit more about the names you are considering?

Perfect Babies' Names is an essential resource for all parents-to-be. Taking a close look at over 3,000 names, it not only tells you each name's meaning and history, it also tells you which famous people have shared it over the years and how popular – or unpopular – it is now. With tips on how to make a shortlist and advice for avoiding unfortunate nicknames, *Perfect Babies' Names* is the ultimate one-stop guide.

The *Perfect* series is a range of practical guides that give clear and straightforward advice on everything from getting your first job to choosing your baby's name. Written by experienced authors offering tried-and-tested tips, each book contains all you need to get it right first time.

BOOKS

Perfect Best Man

George Davidson

All you need to know

- Do you want to make sure you're a great best man?
- Do you want to make the groom glad he chose you?
- Do you need some guidance on your role and responsibilities?

Perfect Best Man is an indispensable guide to every aspect of the best man's role. Covering everything from organising the stag night to making sure the big day runs according to plan, it walks you through exactly what you need to do and gives great advice about getting everything done with the least possible fuss. With checklists to make sure you have it all covered, troubleshooting sections for when things go wrong, and a unique chapter on choosing and organising the ushers, *Perfect Best Man* has everything you need to make sure you rise to the occasion.

BOOKS

Order more titles in the *Perfect* series
from your local bookshop, or have them delivered
direct to your door by Bookpost.

☐ Perfect Answers to Interview Questions	Max Eggert	9781905211722	£7.99
☐ Perfect Babies' Names	Rosalind Fergusson	9781905211661	£5.99
☐ Perfect Calorie Counting	Kate Santon	9781847945181	£6.99
☐ Perfect CV	Max Eggert	9781905211739	£7.99
☐ Perfect Interview	Max Eggert	9781905211746	£7.99
☐ Perfect Numerical Test Results	Joanna Moutafi and Ian Newcombe	9781905211333	£7.99
☐ Perfect Personality Profiles	Helen Baron	9781905211821	£7.99
☐ Perfect Psychometric Test Results	Joanna Moutafi and Ian Newcombe	9781905211678	£7.99
☐ Perfect Pub Quiz	David Pickering	9781905211692	£6.99
☐ Perfect Punctuation	Steven Curtis	9781905211685	£5.99
☐ Perfect Readings for Weddings	Jonathan Law	9781905211098	£6.99
☐ Perfect Wedding Planning	Cherry Chappell	9781905211104	£5.99
☐ Perfect Wedding Speeches and Toasts	George Davidson	9781905211777	£5.99

Free post and packing
Overseas customers allow £2 per paperback

Phone: 01624 677237

Post: Random House Books
c/o Bookpost, PO Box 29, Douglas, Isle of Man IM99 1BQ

Fax: 01624 670 923

email: bookshop@enterprise.net

Cheques (payable to Bookpost) and credit cards accepted

Prices and availability subject to change without notice.
Allow 28 days for delivery.
When placing your order, please state if you do not
wish to receive any additional information.

www.rbooks.co.uk